COLDS & FLU
A Clinical
Doctor/Patient
Manual
by Dr. Richard Schulze

TABLE OF CONTENTS

INTRODUCTION
TO THIS MANUAL

In my clinic laboratory every year around August, I would always start making plenty of Cold and Flu Herbal Medicines. I knew that it was never a matter of "if" my patients would get a cold or flu—it was really a matter of "*when*" my patients would get infected and sick. Sure, a few of my patients, *the healthy elite*, who followed my good health advice, ate clean and healthy food, exercised, used their Foundational Herbal Formulae on a regular basis and did their quarterly Detox programs, well, many of them "dodged the bullet" and stopped getting wintertime colds and flu completely. In fact, most of my "well-behaved" patients that lived a healthy lifestyle rarely got sick at all. But, for the rest of my regular, "not-so-perfect" patients, getting a cold, an upper-respiratory infection or even influenza was a normal fall or winter experience (as with most people worldwide).

So sure enough, every September, patients and their children would start coming into my clinic to be treated for colds and influenza. It is one of the few things in life that you can still count on: that you, a family member, a loved one, or some of your friends or co-workers will get infected with a bacteria or virus this fall, winter or spring.

I guess that my big point right here on the first page of this book is… If we know this is going to happen and we are probably going to get infected, then it just makes great common sense to get prepared and stay prepared, so that when it does happen, instead of getting our butts kicked, we can "open a can of natural whoop-ass" on this alien invader and stop it dead in its tracks. That is what this manual is all about!

I could have written a few thousand pages about colds, flu, bacteria, viruses and immunology alone, not including the thousands of Natural Healing remedies and routines that I know for preventing and treating colds and influenza. In fact, I often taught Immunology classes and seminars in college and I love telling students about the almost magical internal self-repairing and self-healing cosmos that we call the immune system. But, I also love keeping things simple and to the point. I love quick-start instructions, quick-reference guides, trouble-shooting charts, fix-it algorithms and simplified books. I like to quickly skip to the section that I need, see what I need to do, then DO IT and FIX IT! That way, I can get back to having fun. So, at the beginning of each chapter I also added a Quick Reference Chart of the specific Treatment Programs and Herbal Medicines for that section, so you can quickly see exactly what you need to do.

For the most part in this manual, I keep the stories short and get right to the "fix it" parts. The stories I have included are important and they are for your illumination, to help you better understand the points I am making. I also need to wash your brain of much of the medical and scientific nonsense regarding all aspects of colds and influenza that you have been polluted, poisoned and brainwashed with since childhood. As you will see, much of what you have heard about everything from fevers to flu shots is wrong. DEAD WRONG!

This manual is also a work in progress that I started way back in the early 1970s. Actually, some of it I learned in the late 1960s. I would use this information in my clinic on simple printed handouts and booklets that I would give to each of my patients to assist them and provide them with many ways to PREVENT getting a cold or flu infection. And, if they were already sick, well, there are hundreds of natural ways to treat even the worst cold or flu, without going to the doctor or the hospital emergency room, and without getting flu shots or taking antibiotics or even any over-the-counter drugs.

This year, over forty years later, I am still adding to this manual! This manual is my life's work so far—a compilation of my most effective natural treatments and my most powerful herbal medicines for treating colds and influenza.

So, PLEASE learn a few of the natural programs in this book and stock up on a few of the foods and herbal medicines that I mention. If you get even a little prepared, you can turn that "3 to 4-week cold" *that paralyzes you in bed* or "the cough from hell" *that never goes away* or "the flu that keeps coming back" *all winter long*, into a few days of "fun and aggressive Natural Healing purification routines" that will leave you feeling not only physically refreshed, cleaner and stronger, but also emotionally empowered. You'll feel EMPOWERED because you didn't have to run to the emergency room or doctor for more antibiotics. You will discover in reading this manual that learning a little bit more about your body and how to assist it in healing itself of a cold or flu, not only saves you lots of pain and suffering, but it also saves you lots of money too. Oh yeah, and it's fun!

Stay Healthy My Friends,

Dr. Schulze

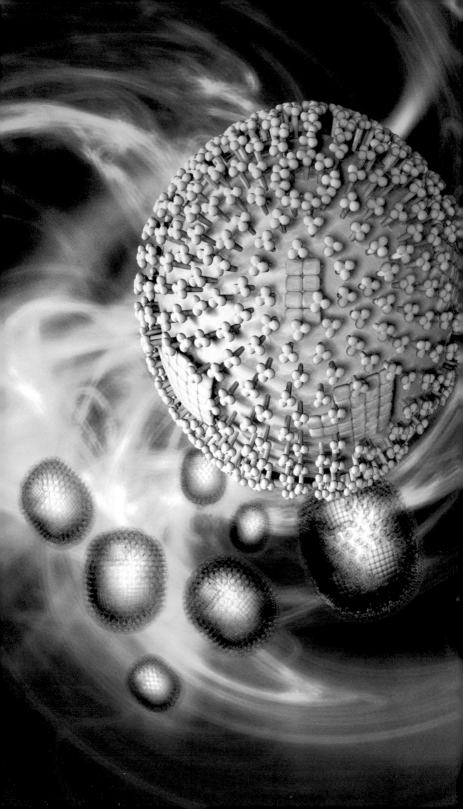

CHAPTER 1
WHAT ARE COLDS AND INFLUENZA?

All colds, upper-respiratory tract infections, influenza, stuffed-up sinuses, sore throats, swollen tonsils and adenoids, coughs, fevers and lung congestion—ALL infections—are thought to be caused by a type of micro-organism, that is sometimes called a pathogen. A pathogen simply means "disease-causing" while another name often used is simply "germ." Whatever we call these *things* that cause colds and influenza, most people seem to agree that they are actually some type of bacteria or virus that are responsible for everything from colds and influenza to strep throat, pneumonia and meningitis.

While colds can be caused by various viruses and bacteria, influenza is caused by viruses only. Influenza or the "flu" is a viral infection of the respiratory tract caused by many different viral strains. These viruses live INSIDE your body's cells, eating them for food. This is sometimes why viruses are referred to as "intracellular parasites."

Now, as a doctor, I must tell you that after sitting with people for decades and observing them, there are always additional emotional and spiritual causes for every "dis-ease." But having said that, I think it is also fairly safe to say that what we call colds or flu are actually viral or bacterial infections, *if we want to get all scientific about it.*

And, it's fairly easy to tell if you have one, as you usually get a fever, a runny or stuffed-up nose, a sore throat, a cough or lung congestion and a headache or body aches. And, the most common names attached to these infections are usually colds, the flu, influenza, upper-respiratory infections, rhino-virus and pneumonia. But remember, there are 1,001 different *germs* causing these infections and also 1,001 names we call these infections. They are all slightly different in the symptoms that they produce. Some are very mild, like the recent H1N1 Swine Flu, while others are much more intense, more painful, more aggressive and more dangerous.

Why is there a Cold and Flu Season?

Bacterial and viral infections actually happen all year long, but it is true that most people are infected between September and April. There are a few reasons for this. The main one is that during the fall, winter and early spring, people are more confined to their homes and/or offices with less ventilation, less fresh air and more closed windows. Since bacterial and viral infections are commonly spread by infected saliva and mucous "droplets" from sick, infected people coughing and sneezing, the less fresh airflow we have and the more we are huddled together *breathing the same air*, the more that we are exposed to much more bacterial and viral contamination. This makes it much easier to *spread* the infection from person to person. During this time of year, when one person gets sick, they can spread the infection to hundreds of others in a matter of hours, depending on the level of confinement. So, one of the best ways to keep from being infected is to stay away from others, especially anyone who is coughing or sneezing.

There are also many other reasons that the cold and flu epidemic happens at this time of year, from the fact that the weather is colder to that fact that we get less sunlight. You will see these and many other additional factors that lower your immune resistance and make you much more susceptible to *catching* a cold or flu explained later in this manual in the section called **"9 Effective Cold & Flu Prevention Tips"**.

The Only American Epidemic

Influenza is the only reoccurring epidemic in America and most highly civilized countries that still exists, **KILLING A MINIMUM OF 40,000 AMERICAN MEN, WOMEN AND CHILDREN EVERY SINGLE YEAR**, and many more worldwide. Some years in America, it kills over double that amount.

In fact, Americans get over **ONE BILLION cold and influenza infections** every year between the months of September and April, **that is at a rate of FOUR MILLION people getting infected with colds and influenza EVERY DAY.**

Collectively, Americans will also spend over **200 million days** in bed this year and lose **100 million days** of work, adding up to **$10 BILLION in lost wages!**

THE AVERAGE AMERICAN GETS OVER THREE COLD AND INFLUENZA INFECTIONS during the six winter months. **250,000 can be hospitalized in an average year.** If you just walk into the hospital emergency room with a cold, the **initial cost is over $500** without any treatment—just to fill out the forms. And if you **have pneumonia, it will cost you about $15,000.**

Again, over 40,000 people will die just from a mild influenza season this year alone, not including the number that will die from colds and upper-respiratory infections. If we got a bad one again like the Spanish Flu that killed 50 MILLION people across the planet, MILLIONS of Americans will die.

Recently, I have been stating that Americans have been in an uproar about the 5,000 men and women that were killed in the Iraq War over the past decade, and as far as I am concerned, that is 5,000 too many. **But… 10 times that number will be killed, GUARANTEED, in only a few months this winter,** and we hardly speak of it. In fact, more Americans will die this winter from influenza than all the soldiers who died in the entire Vietnam War!

Personally, I consider colds and influenza *murderers* of epidemic proportions that have killed the young and old and have made hundreds of thousands extremely ill. So, I respect them and I never underestimate the potential lethality of the cold and influenza season. This is why I always prefer the aggressive approach. As you will come to understand, I am famous for my intensive Natural Healing routines, and the concentrated potency of my herbal medicines has scared most other naturopaths and herbalists, not to mention my dosages. My routines and medicines are no different when it comes to the common cold or influenza and I cannot overstate the importance of being prepared to kick its ass, before it kicks yours!

Viral "Drifting" and "Shifting"

You can get viral influenza more than once a year and many people get it every year. This is because, like bacteria, viruses change and mutate. These changes are often referred to as "drifting" and "shifting."

When a virus mutates gradually, this is referred to as a "drift." This constant changing enables the virus to evade your immune system's defenses, go unrecognized and infect you again. When a virus changes quickly, this is called a "shift." This is an abrupt change where the virus mutates very quickly into a new subtype. Because of this "drifting" and "shifting", it is possible for you to get the flu every year, even two or three times in one year.

Is It Important to Know Which Type of Infection You Have?

NO! It doesn't really matter, simply because in Natural Healing, we treat them all the same. (See page 22 for "Why Natural Treatment is Different.")

When you are using the modern medical approach and are "trying to poison yourself well" with highly dangerous and toxic flu shots, (see page 122 for "What's Wrong with the Flu Shot?") antibiotics or anti-viral drugs, it is *supposedly* extremely important to use the right drug for the right bug. This is actually an impossible task, due to many factors, such as the natural "drifting" and "shifting" of influenza viruses. Another reason is that the tests themselves are highly inaccurate and take a long time. With the flu shot, for example, the species of flu has to be "predicted" a year in advance for what specific bug they think is coming the following year. This is why billions are spent every year on flu shots that many experts in the medical and scientific community think are a total folly. Recently, top medical texts and FDA advisors have stated that **it is doubtful if treating people with flu shots and antibiotics has any positive affect at all.**

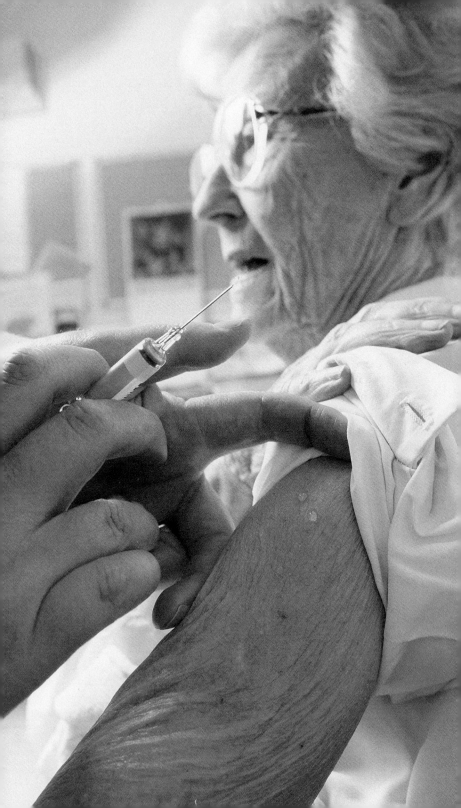

CHAPTER 2
WHAT'S WRONG WITH ANTIBIOTICS AND FLU SHOTS?

What About Antibiotics?

According to the AMA and most medical experts, antibiotics are absolutely USELESS FOR TREATING influenza (which are viruses), colds (which are usually also a virus—the rhino-virus) and even upper-respiratory tract infections (that are sometimes bacterial). Regardless, antibiotics do not seem to have a positive affect in treating any of them. So, everybody seems to agree that **antibiotics have NO preventative or curing effect on influenza or colds!** Then, why is it that this winter, American medical doctors will literally write millions and millions of prescriptions for antibiotics for their patients with colds and influenza?

Well, there seems to be a few answers for this question.

The first one is money, because this winter alone, drug companies will make billions of dollars selling antibiotics with medical doctors as their "drug dealers and pimps", I mean… "sales force." The pharmaceutical companies who fund a lot of medical research, give a lot of educational and research grants and fund a lot of hospitals will put a lot of direct pressure on the medical doctors to write millions of prescriptions to sell their drugs. It's all about making money.

Second, medical doctors want to make their patients happy, and patients scream, beg for and demand antibiotics. So medical doctors, even though they know antibiotics are useless against colds and flu (and cause other health problems), will write their patients prescriptions for them, just to keep their patients happy. I have had many medical doctors tell me that they want to do the right thing and tell their patients "no", but they have said that their patients will simply find another medical doctor to write the prescription, so they might as well write it and make their patients happy.

According to Dr. Fred Rubin, MD, associate clinical professor of medicine at the University of Pittsburgh and contributor to *The Merck Manual—Home Edition*, **"Not only are antibiotics powerless against the viruses that cause colds and flu, but misuse of antibiotics can actually do more harm than good."**

According to *The Journal of the American Medical Association*, the high rates of antibiotic prescribing and misuse has caused alarming increases in new harmful drug-resistant organisms, like flesh-eating bacteria and other unstoppable and lethal hospital bacteria.

The bottom line is that for treating influenza and colds, DON'T TAKE ANTIBIOTICS!

OK, I won't take antibiotics, but what about a flu shot?

Every year, American pharmaceutical companies are making over 100 million doses of the flu shot. This is big business. Do the math. We're talking BILLIONS and BILLIONS of dollars, all a part of the highly lucrative $2,000,000,000,000.00 a year American Medical Show.

Some medical doctors and hospitals even prescribe general non-specific antiviral drugs, but even the Center for Disease Control warns that this is an **"untested and expensive strategy and could result in large numbers of people getting ill."**

There are hundreds of known influenza viruses and over 200 common ones. They never come alone, and each year we see a new and unique blend of many old viruses, along with some new, mutated ones. To give you an idea of the folly of viral prediction (which by the way has never been done correctly), let's take a look at the past viral cocktails that have been given as flu shots. Since it takes months to manufacture influenza shots, the viral mix has to be a guess or prediction of what is *thought* will be arriving the *next* flu season. Again, NONE of these flu shot predictions has ever been accurate to what actually arrived the following flu season.

▶ In 2002, the flu shot was a blend of the A/Moscow/10/99 (H3N2), B/Victoria/504/2000, A/New Caledonia/20/99 (H1N1), A/Panama/2007/99 (H3N2), B/Johannesburg/05/99, B/Guangdong/120/2000, and B/Sichuan/379/99.

▶ In 2003, the toxic viral flu shot blend included A/New Caledonia/20/99-like (H1N1), A/Moscow/10/99-like (H3N2) and B/Hong Kong/330/2001-like viruses. For the A/Moscow/10/99-like (H3N2) virus, U.S. manufacturers used the antigenically equivalent A/Panama/2007/99 (H3N2) virus and for the B/Hong Kong/330/2001-like virus, they used either B/Hong Kong/330/2001 or the antigenically equivalent virus B/Hong Kong/1434/2002. These viruses were used because of their growth properties and because they are representative of circulating A (H3N2) and B viruses.

▶ In 2004, the toxic viral cocktail included A/Moscow/10/99 (H3N2-like), A/New Caledonia/20/99 (H1N1-like), and B/Hong Kong/330/2001-like antigens (for the A/Moscow/10/99 [H3N2]-like antigen, manufacturers used the antigenically equivalent A/Panama/2007/99 [H3N2] virus, and for the B/Hong Kong/330/2001-like antigen, manufacturers used either B/Hong Kong/330/2001 or the antigenically equivalent B/Hong Kong/1434/2002.)

▶ In 2005, the toxic flu shot is a blend of A/New Caledonia/20/99-like (H1N1), A/California/7/2004-like (H3N2) or the antigenically equivalent A/New York/55/2004, and the B/Shanghai/361/2002-like viruses (or the antigenically equivalent B/Jilin/20/2003 or B/Jiangsu/10/2003 viruses).

As I stated above, medical doctors literally spin the dial and guess at which viruses they think might come around the following year, because the vaccines have to be prepared up to a year in advance. Even if they were exactly right with their guess as to which virus blend to put in the shot, and even if they got the right proportions, that still doesn't account for the new kids on the block! Influenza vaccine history shows that often, even if they guessed right, the virus mutates during the year, rendering the "flu shot" impotent. You still end up getting sick with the new mutated virus.

Injecting blends of viruses into your body can also be very dangerous. I remember the Swine Flu vaccine. It made people sicker than the Swine Flu itself and left others dead. This was because influenza vaccines can cause Guillain-Barre Syndrome—the immediate inflammatory destruction of the nerve sheath which causes rapid paralysis. This left many who got the Swine Flu vaccine paralyzed. All vaccines can also cause life-threatening and lethal allergic reactions.

Therefore, the only safe and effective defense to influenza is having a strong offense. In other words, a strong immune system that can kill and make antibodies for any virus that ever existed and any new ones that mutate. The key to a strong immune system is a healthy lifestyle. It also doesn't hurt to have some potent herbal tonics around.

Who Is Most At Risk?

Up until a few years ago, "flu shots" were only recommended for those over 65 years of age. But, because of the exploding viral epidemics, the shot is now suggested for anyone at high risk. About 100 million Americans are considered to be at high risk. These high-risk individuals include anyone over 50 years old, young children, or people of any age with a chronic disease of the heart, lungs (like asthma and bronchitis), kidneys, diabetes, or those with an immune deficiency. If you don't fall into one of those groups, that doesn't make you immune. The Spanish Flu killed tens of thousands of healthy and strong young men 20 to 35 years of age.

More Facts About Viruses

This year the influenza virus will spread across America, and government agencies like the World Health Organization, the Center for Disease Control and many others will collaborate and recommend what the following year's flu cocktail shot should be. After reviewing their data, 100 MILLION FLU SHOTS will be produced by three multi-billion dollar manufacturers.

Right now, I want to give you two flu vaccination statistics and thoughts that you won't get from your local medical doctor who is selling you or even giving you a "free" flu shot… trust me, there is no "free" and somebody paid for it.

FACT #1: If you had five consecutive flu shots in any decade, your chance of getting Alzheimer's disease is 10 TIMES HIGHER. This is partially due to the mercury and aluminum that is in every flu shot (and most childhood shots) that builds up in the brain and causes cognitive dysfunction and disease. This is partially why the rate of Alzheimer's disease is skyrocketing.

FACT #2: "There is no evidence that any influenza vaccine thus far developed is effective in preventing or mitigating any attack of influenza. The producers of these vaccines know that they are worthless, but they go on selling them anyway." — Dr. J. Anthony Morris, former Chief Vaccine Control Officer at the FDA

Poisons In The Typical Flu Vaccine:

▸ Ethylene Glycol — Used as automobile anti-freeze

▸ Carbolic Acid — A toxic, caustic poison

▸ Formaldehyde — Embalming fluid that causes cancer

▸ Aluminum — Known to cause Alzheimer's disease, seizures and cancer

> ▶ Mercury   Found in the vaccine preservative, Thimerosal. Extremely toxic heavy metal that kills brain, nerve and immune cells. Its use in vaccines is linked to many childhood brain and nerve diseases.

The Problem With All Vaccinations Is Not A New One

"Several of my personal friends now have cancer, some of them have died from it. I have inquired into the probable cause of the serious increase of this horrible disease. I believe, as do many other physicians, that cancer is due to impregnating the blood with impure matter and it is obvious that the largest method by which this is done is vaccinations and revaccinations." — J.S. Preston, M.D.

"The increase in cancer has jumped four times higher in just the short time since vaccinations have been made compulsory. This terrible increase is one of the most unsatisfactory features of the new government Vaccination Act." — M. Hibbert, M.D., Secretary of the Government Medical Board

"Vaccinations are how cancer is spread." — *The London Hospital Gazette*

"I am thoroughly convinced that the recent great increase in cancer is directly due to vaccination. I have written my report to several members of Parliament and invited them to the hospital to witness the dismal results of the Vaccination Act for themselves." — William Forbes, M.D., Medical Director, St. Saviours Cancer Hospital, Regents Park, London, England

All of the above statements were reported and entered into the esteemed *Medical Record*, Volume 31, published in New York, USA, January 11th, 1887. **THAT'S 1887!**

This report was a warning to the medical profession in the United States. Great Britain had begun their Compulsory Vaccination Act and the incidence of cancer and many other diseases was skyrocketing. American medical doctors did not heed this warning, nor did the British themselves. Since then, the incidence of cancer has increased OVER 30 TIMES!

Now, more than 120 years later...

▶ In the U.S. from July 1990 to November 1993, the FDA counted a total of 54,072 adverse reactions following vaccination. It also admitted that this number represented only 10% of the real total, because doctors were refusing to report vaccine injuries. In other words, adverse reactions for this period exceeded half a million.

▶ The FDA recently reported that 90% of doctors do not report vaccine reactions. In the seven years from 1990 to 1997, more than $802 million had been awarded for hundreds of injuries and deaths caused by mandated vaccines. Thousands of cases are still pending, but for the majority of claimants there is no money available.

More STARTLING FACTS About Vaccinations

▶ In 1977, Dr. Jonas Salk (inventor of the Salk polio vaccine) testified along with other scientists that most (87%) of the polio cases which have occurred in the U.S. since the early 1970s probably were the by-product of the polio vaccine itself.

▶ In the U.S., the cost of a single DPT shot rose from 11 cents in 1982 to $15.00 in 1992. The vaccine company is putting away $12.00 per shot to cover legal costs and damages paid to parents of the brain-damaged children who die after vaccination.

▶ Children die at a rate of eight times greater than average within three days of getting a DPT (Diphtheria-Pertussis-Tetanus) shot.

▶ There was never, EVER a case of autism in children before childhood vaccinations were used.

Maybe The Worst Yet, Drugs Don't Educate Your Immune System!

KILLING DISEASES with harsh and dangerous chemical drugs is, at best, only a temporary quick fix. Your immune system is left uneducated so the same disease will return again, and usually with a vengeance the second time around. This is why people who try to KILL a cold and flu with drugs usually have constant reoccurring colds and flu. This is also why after a medical doctor cuts, burns or poisons out a person's cancer, it almost always returns. The body and immune system were never educated, no "real" healing took place, only part of a disease was killed and the person is still living a cold, flu or even cancer-creating lifestyle.

CURING DISEASES with a healthy lifestyle creates a strong and educated immune system, so you don't have a reoccurrence of the same problem later. Your body was supported with great nutrition and cleansing and it figured out how to HEAL you all by itself. THIS IS THE ONLY TRUE HEALING: SELF-HEALING. Diseases are the by-product of a faulty lifestyle, therefore the only real cure, the only real healing for anything, is creating a healthier lifestyle and letting your body heal you.

HEALTH is the only true healing or cure for ANYTHING, especially the common cold and influenza. And only your body can create health, by you living a healthy lifestyle. Your body can heal itself of ANYTHING—all it needs is your help. Living a healthy lifestyle will also prevent future disease before it even starts, by building you a strong, powerful and protective immune system.

The Pandemic That Never Was

The Invisible 2009-2010 Swine Flu Pandemic

The recent headline of the British Daily Mail newspaper stated that £1.2 BILLION, or about $1.8 BILLION, had been spent on Swine Flu vaccines in Britain and it is estimated that at most, only 26 lives were spared. That means that it cost £46 MILLION, or about **$70 MILLION per person saved.** They have a reason to be very upset.

The people of Britain were, in fact, livid (as they should be) that in these hard economic times, why so much money was wasted on an influenza vaccine that was never needed. The British Government has been launching numerous queries and creating committees to investigate this scandal and try to discover how and why this very expensive and very useless flu vaccine folly happened.

From the reports so far, everyone is blaming the World Health Organization for whipping up a massive pandemic hysteria needlessly. In fact, the Chief Medical Officer of Britain, Dr. Liam Donaldson, warned that over 65,000 people could be dead in Britain in just a few months from the Swine Flu. However, the Swine Flu actually ended up claiming only 342 lives, which was a lot less than even a "normal" flu season.

As the dust settled and the scandal heightened, it was uncovered that the majority of medical officers in the British Government and also in the American Government (the ones who highly advised to manufacture almost $2 BILLION worth of vaccine for Britain, plus BILLIONS and BILLIONS of dollars more for the United States) were also on the payroll or paid board members of the companies that made the vaccine and received the $2 BILLION in taxpayers' money.

And, the H1N1 Swine Flu "Pandemic" never happened!

The 1976 Swine Flu Fiasco

When I was warning my customers in 2009 that this Swine Flu Pandemic was probably never going to materialize, the American Government was whipping up the hysteria and fear by predicting wintertime death tolls in the hundreds of thousands and a full-blown influenza pandemic.

I told customers that the EXACT same thing had happened with the American Government's Swine Flu Pandemic scare in 1976. I remember it very well. A few soldiers at Fort Dix in New Jersey supposedly got the Swine Flu (who knows if they ever actually did?) The next thing we knew, there was a massive Swine Flu Pandemic alert, with a massive public-service campaign and commercials, all over the television, newspapers, magazines and radio, urging Americans to get the Swine Flu vaccine. In fact, look it up on the Internet. Just type in 1970s Swine Flu and you will see the videos of all of these ridiculous public service commercials that are now called "government propaganda". This flu is even now referred to as the "Swine Flu Fiasco" or the "Swine Flu Debacle".

The government warned that we were going to have a Swine Flu Pandemic back then, and that millions would be infected and hundreds of thousands or Americans would die. So they manufactured a Swine Flu vaccine, and *pushed* it on the majority of Americans. **It was the greatest mass-influenza vaccination effort in American history, with 40 million Americans getting injected with the vaccine in just the first three months of the flu season: October, November and December.** But on December 16th, the Federal Government was put under pressure to halt their Swine Flu vaccine program. Why?

For two reasons: First, the Swine Flu never came! Second, **PEOPLE WERE DYING FROM THE VACCINE,** not the Swine Flu. Also, many others were getting very sick from the vaccine itself. Just one of the diseases the vaccine had caused was Guillain-Barre Syndrome, which paralyzes you. So as it turned out, **the only deaths and disease from the 1976 Swine Flu, were from the toxic and poisonous vaccine and the American Government's successful mass-immunization program.**

So Back To The Present

This is why just after the American Government, the White House staff and the WHO all announced that we were in for a huge death toll in the fall of 2009, I went over to London (the supposed epicenter of the European Swine Flu breakout, ground zero, so to speak) to see what was happening. I hit the streets with my video camera and barely found anyone who had the Swine Flu. And the few I did find, well, they thought it was just a joke, a very mild flu, much milder than the seasonal influenza. You can still see this Swine Flu video at my website.

The Great Swine Flu Swindle

SUMMER 2009, WHAT THEY SAID:

▸ CDC and WHO declare WORLDWIDE PANDEMIC due to Swine Flu H1N1-Virus.

▸ A White House report estimated 100,000 or more deaths in the United States, due to Swine Flu.

SUMMER 2009, WHAT DR. SCHULZE SAID:

"MOST viral threats never materialize and never amount to much more than just a few more cases of the flu." — Dr. Schulze

WHAT THEY ARE SAYING NOW:

▸ Dr. Wolfgang Wodarg, Head of Health at the Council of Europe, has now come out and accused the vaccine manufacturers of INFLUENCING both his organization's and the WHO's decision to declare a pandemic.

▸ He and many of his colleagues in Europe have branded the H1N1 outbreak as "one of the greatest medical scandals of the century."

▸ The U.S. has spent BILLIONS of tax dollars to purchase 250 million doses of H1N1 vaccine!

"As I told my customers, this is just another medical-induced scare to sell a trillion dollars worth of drugs around the world." — Dr. Schulze

Why Natural Treatment is Different

The reason why we don't need to know exactly which specific bug you have been infected with is actually quite simple. It is the same reason why in Natural Healing we don't need to know exactly what disease you have either.

To make it really simple, we should look at the old philosophy of "Focus on the Good to Eliminate the Bad." This is basically what we do: Just get really healthy and your "dis-eases" will simply vanish and we didn't even have to pay attention to them. Look at my clinical sign that now hangs in my pharmacy store in California that states, "You can heal yourself of ANYTHING. All you have to do is to STOP doing what made you sick in the first place, and START doing things that will Create Powerful Health, and your dis-ease will simply vanish!"

Look, I think I am a pretty bright guy, but I never let my ego get so out of control that I think that I know exactly what is wrong with people—their particular disease, their specific illness—or that I understand the trillions of functions of the human body. **What I DO KNOW is that your own body, if given half a chance and if given the opportunity, will heal itself of ANYTHING. THIS IS WHAT IT WAS DESIGNED TO DO! So all that I have to do as your doctor is educate you in ways to get really, really healthy. Then your body will discover exactly what is wrong and will also know exactly which medicines to make and exactly how to fix you. After all, in the first week of medical school you learn that your body is a self-repairing and self-healing machine and is designed to constantly heal and repair itself. It knows how to do this better than any medical doctor, hospital or pharmaceutical company!**

With Natural Healing you get clean, healthy and strong, and let your body make all of the right decisions and specific medicines it needs (as you will see in the next segment of this manual). Again, I will simply help you to create the healthiest lifestyle and environment possible for you, to promote health and let your body do what it does best, which is fight infection and heal you.

Sure, I will suggest a few natural and extremely powerful immune system turbo-charging agents like Echinacea and some highly potent non-specific infection and disease killers like Garlic. But, I won't even begin to bullshit myself or you that I am smart enough to discover which of the trillions of bacteria or viruses you might have, and then mix up extremely concentrated, toxic, smart-bomb chemicals to kill it (that would probably backfire and kill YOU instead). I will leave the diagnosis and cure up to your immune system, your body and God.

Your Immune System

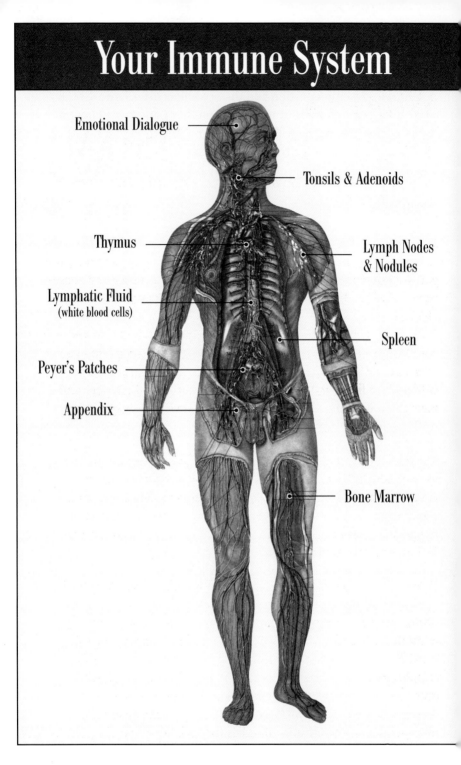

Emotional Dialogue

Tonsils & Adenoids

Thymus

Lymph Nodes & Nodules

Lymphatic Fluid
(white blood cells)

Spleen

Peyer's Patches

Appendix

Bone Marrow

CHAPTER 3
WHAT IS YOUR IMMUNE SYSTEM:
Where is it hiding, how does it work and what does it do for YOU?

Your body is going to make you your own personal cold or flu shot, regardless of what you or I do. My job is simply to make sure you are not getting in its way with any health-disabling or disease-promoting activities, like consuming junk food, sugar, tobacco, alcohol, etc. I am also going to *assist* your body to make its own "medicine" by supplying you with super nutrition and also *nudge* your body to do this faster, better and stronger, by supplying you with natural immune boosting plants that will supercharge your cold and flu fighting defenses and drive them into high gear and have them working at their peak performance. This way you get well in a few hours, not weeks!

The reason your body can heal you of colds and influenza and make its own natural "medicines" is because it has an immune system. A system that is designed to have constant surveillance over you, watching for any possible invaders, and then at the first detection of you being invaded by any harmful pathogen, it turns on its many defense systems to protect you.

Your immune system is a unique body system, because it is actually comprised of numerous organs, tissues, systems, blood cells, fluids, nodes, nodules, bones and other pieces and parts all over your body. But, when they are all working together it can stop anything; it can kill anything. Some of its parts are your white blood cells, lymphocytes (like T-cells) educated in your thymus to kill, while other T-cells are designed to communicate information and to do various other jobs. And B-cells, which use different surface immunoglobulin to create antibodies (basically very specific poisons to kill very specific bacteria, virus, whatever). And, your lymphatic fluid, immune fluids (like interferon and interleukin) and organs (like your thymus and your spleen, lymphatic nodes and nodules). There are also lymphatic aggregations (like your appendix, tonsils, adenoids and Peyer's patches) along with red bone marrow, etc. There are even missing links in your immune system that science knows are there, but doesn't have a clue exactly where they are. An example is your B-cells. As ridiculous as science can be, they are actually named after an organ in a bird that humans don't even have, the *Bursa of Fabriscus*. How and where these B-cells are educated in humans is a big mystery that most medical doctors don't like to talk about, simply because they have no idea. So a very big, complex combination of bits and parts and even some mysterious unknown factors and voila... we have an immune system!

You Are What You THINK!

Finally, if you are feeling ignorant even after this very simple explanation, *don't go there!* Because we now know that your immune system is listening. Since it has been discovered that your immune cells have neuro-peptide receptors on them, and neuro-peptides are the chemicals that you make in your brain whenever you have any thoughts—like love, bliss, hate, whatever—it is now known that your own immune system is listening to you, and *listening* to what you are thinking (like J. Edgar Hoover in the 1950s).

Beyond that, since everything in your body does something for a reason, then your immune system isn't just listening, it's also *reacting*. Oh no… does this mean that our immune system is actually *listening* and also *reacting* to our emotional dialog? It does!

So a big part of healing colds and flu naturally is staying POSITIVE. This is yet another reason that this book is so important, to have me empower you with education, enlightenment and illumination—and plenty of natural and herbal tools—so the next time you get a cold or flu, you can stay very positive and look at it as an *opportunity* for your body to do some detoxifying, cleansing, immune boosting and health building!

The bottom line is that in the first few weeks of medical school you learn that the human body is designed to heal and repair itself, unlike any machine. Well, it is the immune system that does a big part of this healing and repairing.

A Brief And Simplified Description Of Your Immune Response

NOTE: YOU DO NOT HAVE TO KNOW ANY OF THE FOLLOWING INFORMATION TO BE WELL AND CAN SKIP RIGHT TO CHAPTER FOUR. But, for those students of Natural Healing, and those patients who want a better understanding of what is going on inside of their body, I will give you my anatomical and metabolic description of your immune system. I have done my best to simplify it, limit the use of "ten dollar" words and explain it in a way that just makes good common sense.

So here is the simplified anatomy and physiology of one of the most complex systems in the human body; the Immune System…

Why Anatomy And Physiology?

Patients and students often asked me, "Why do you always discuss anatomy and physiology?" The answer is quite simple. My clinical experience taught me that most people are pretty darn smart (regardless of what medical doctors think) and have good common sense. My patients were perfectly capable of understanding where their body parts are and what they do.

Look, medical doctors have a hard sell. Their job is not easy. They have to convince you to do something that could kill you, that will be painful if not excruciating, horrifying, disfiguring and debilitating, and that will cost you tens of thousands of dollars, if not your life savings. If they didn't use fear and pressure, who would do something as crazy as this?

To further ensure the success of their con job, they use huge words often from foreign or dead languages like Greek and Latin, and rarely explain things in a way that the average person could understand them. **Often a patient's biggest mistake is to not realize that medical doctors, drugs and hospitals are a big, profit-oriented business** (actually the biggest money-making business in the United States). I am not saying that every medical doctor is a conman, but the system they work for is definitely crooked and designed to try and get your entire nest egg before you die.

On the other hand, my life's crusade started as a teenager when medical doctors succeeded in killing both of my parents and then almost killed me.

I literally saved my life by taking my healthcare into my own hands. So, my natural instinct and healing crusade is to teach people how to heal themselves naturally, without doctors, drugs or hospitals. To teach people that their body can and will heal itself of ANYTHING, ANY DISEASE, if they would just be willing to create a healthy enough lifestyle. I teach people how to create such powerful health, that disease literally retreats, goes away and disappears.

So back to the original question... "Why Anatomy And Physiology?"

I find that the average person, given a few hours, can easily understand plenty about where their organs are, how they work and what they do. And when a person understands this, they can then understand what their medical doctor was talking about.

More importantly, with a little knowledge of anatomy and physiology my patients could easily understand that the sanest, common sense FIRST APPROACH (before choosing medical intervention) is to adjust your lifestyle to STOP doing what causes the organ to be sick. This reduces the inflammation and immediately starts the healing process. Next, we START doing some programs that clear the organ's blockage and congestion, feed it nutrition and get it cleaned out and running better. What my patients quickly discovered was that their pain and discomfort would be gone in days, if not hours. Soon their illness would be gone, too, and they would be healthy. A little knowledge is a powerful healing tool.

Your immune system is a very unique system, because it is comprised of many different types of organs, tissues, cells and fluids and these various parts are located all over your body.

Your Immune System

The major components of your immune system are:

▸ **LYMPHATIC FLUID,** which contains the many different **IMMUNE BLOOD CELLS** (like B-cells and T-cells).

▸ **LYMPHATIC SYSTEM,** in which the lymphatic fluid flows, that includes **VESSELS, DUCTS, NODES** and **NODULES.**

▸ **BONE MARROW,** where all cells and all immune cells come from.

▸ **LYMPHOID AGGREGATIONS** like the **TONSILS, ADENOIDS, PEYER'S PATCHES** and the **APPENDIX** that are the immune system's communication organs, and may also be where the B-cells are educated.

▸ **THYMUS,** which is where the T-cells are educated.

▸ **SPLEEN,** which is not only a blood storage organ "tank", but is loaded with immune cells, like a meeting hall where they can all talk and communicate with each other.

This system has one main objective, to protect you from harmful alien invaders or self-mutation.

These invaders are often referred to as antigens (anti-creation or life) or pathogens (disease-creation) or just germs. These harmful micro-organisms include bacteria, viruses, fungi, pollen, cancer cells, etc. Your self-mutating cells can be anything from old worn-out and dead red blood cells to cancer. Any substance that is not you, not self, or worn-out parts, are dealt with by your immune system. It is killed and/or eaten and disposed of. It's that simple.

Your immune system has two major jobs: Surveillance and Action.

It constantly checks your blood and body for any invaders and if it detects any, it goes into action. The surveillance is achieved by the constant checking of your digestive tract, lungs, blood, virtually every cell of your body. Almost all parts of your immune system have the ability to survey and kill.

The action it takes to destroy, neutralize and eliminate invading micro-organisms is fascinating and complex, and science is far from knowing it all.

I literally spent years studying this system only to discover that many authors and their books disagree on how it works—and even if they agree, their explanation is so complex you would need your accountant, a Philadelphia lawyer and a NASA rocket scientist to figure out what the heck they are talking about. So basically, I decided to create my own description and even more medical blasphemy—my own immune system chart—so that you can better understand this amazing system.

On page 34 is a chart I designed that represents your blood cells and the various cells of your immune system. This is only one aspect of your immune system, but it is a very important aspect of it. The anatomy and physiology of your blood and immune cells is very complicated and volumes and volumes of medical books are spent on just this subject. At the same time, many of my patients were told things about their immune cells that they did not understand, so that is why I designed this chart. My idea was to simplify the subject from a library of medical books down to one page and a few paragraphs.

It is not necessary to know or even understand any of the following to be well, heal your disease and illness and build a powerful immune system—but for those who want a little better idea of what is going on anatomically and metabolically, read on.

Most medical scientists agree that there is one cell that all other blood cells, both white blood cells and red blood cells, are derived from. It is sometimes referred to as a hemocytoblast, meaning hemo = blood / cyto = cell / blast = create, or 'blood-cell-create'. It is also referred to simply as the "stem cell", which is a more popular name in the press these days, especially regarding stem cell research.

This stem cell is found in the bone marrow and develops into either a haemopoietic stem cell or a lymphoid stem cell.

The Haemopoietic Stem Cell

As you can see in my chart (on page 34), this cell creates or turns into all red blood cells. It creates megakaryocytes, which when mixed with thrombopoietin turn into blood platelets, which are a major component of our red blood. It also turns into an erythroid stem cell that combines with erthropoietin to create all erythrocytes or red blood cells.

It also creates the myeloid stem cells that when stimulated by colony stimulating factors turn into some of the most prevalent and powerful white blood immune cells in your body, monocytes and macrophages. They are usually referred to as monocytes when they are present in your blood, and macrophages when in your body tissue. Macrophage literally translates to mean "big eater," and this is exactly what they do. This gluttonous white blood cell gobbles up everything from germs to cancer—it's an eating PacMan pig and saves your life, every minute of every day.

This same myeloid stem cell can also turn into a granulocyte stem cell, which when also mixed with a colony stimulating factor produces the granulocyte immune cells, which are basophils, eosinophils and neutrophils. These powerful immune cells are present both in your blood and in your body's tissues. These important cells have very specific jobs, like killing bacteria and parasites and reducing inflammation.

The Lymphoid Stem Cell

The lymphoid stem cell is the other main cell that the original stem cell creates. It is the mother of all of your immune T-lymphocyte cells and B-lymphocyte cells.

If the lymphoid stem cell is transported in your blood through your thymus, then it is educated there and turned into one of a wide variety of T-cells.

It can either become a T-4 lymphocyte (sometimes called a T-helper cell), a T-8 lymphocyte (sometimes called a T-suppressor cell), a TK-lymphocyte (sometimes called a T-killer cell), or a cytotoxic cell. Scientists are discovering other T-cells all the time.

The lymphoid stem cell can also be educated somewhere else (science has yet to discover where) and turned into a B-lymphocyte cell.

Science doesn't know where this educational process takes place for the B-cell. It was originally called the B-cell because in birds—it is known that it is educated in an organ called the *Bursa of Fabricius*, but humans do not have that organ, so in humans it is still not understood where this B-cell is educated. Some people think it's in the bone marrow, the intestines or one of the lymphoid aggregations like the Peyer's Patches, tonsils or appendix, and possibly even the spleen or the liver. No one really knows. If it happens to be a lymphoid aggregation like the tonsils, adenoids or appendix (and also being that these are very popular organs for medical doctors to cut out of your body), then this could be a great explanation of why Americans have weaker and weaker immune systems and a lack of immune strength and a lack of immune cell education.

On the surface of each B-cell is a substance called immunoglobulin. The B-cell uses different types of surface immunoglobulin to create antibodies, which are designed to kill specific various bacteria, viruses, fungi and other antigens and pathogens.

So How Does This All Work?

Well, first let's forget your blood platelets and red blood cells, because they are your red blood and really not a part of your immune system. So how it all works is when anything like a pathogen (meaning disease-creating, or disease-causing) or just a germ enters your body (this can be anything like a bacteria, virus, fungus, pollen—anything that is not you that can harm you, or just a worn-out part of you), there is a whole complex process of your immune action that takes place.

First off, the monocytes or the macrophages (remember the big eaters) attack viciously to kill and eat up any substance that isn't you. Secondly, your other immune cells from the myeloid stem cell, the granulocytes, the basophils, eosinophils and neutrophils also have their specific jobs to do in killing the invader, whether it's a parasite or bacteria. The T-cells and B-cells work differently, in a much more complex fashion.

The T-lymphocyte cells work together with the B-lymphocyte cells. First off, while the macrophages are off killing the invader immediately, without any thought (they are just lethal killing machines), they also excrete certain immune fluids like interleukin and interferon. The name interferon is simply derived from the word "interfere", as this chemical substance assists the immune cells to interfere with the bacteria and viruses ability to replicate and reproduce. These immune chemicals also activate other immune cells, like T-killer cells; they increase the communication ability between immune cells and even help protect your body's healthy cells that have not been infected, and make them more resistant to the bacteria and virus.

The Basic Cellular Machiner

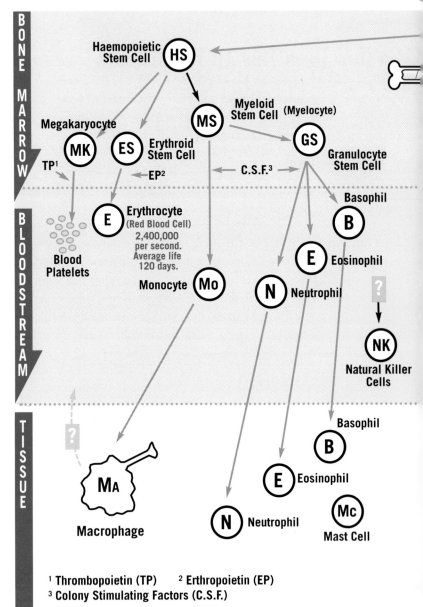

BONE MARROW

Haemopoietic Stem Cell (HS)

Megakaryocyte (MK)

(ES) Erythroid Stem Cell

Myeloid Stem Cell (MS) (Myelocyte)

(GS) Granulocyte Stem Cell

TP[1]

EP[2]

C.S.F.[3]

BLOODSTREAM

(E) Erythrocyte (Red Blood Cell) 2,400,000 per second. Average life 120 days.

Blood Platelets

Monocyte (Mo)

(N) Neutrophil

(E) Eosinophil

Basophil (B)

? (NK) Natural Killer Cells

TISSUE

?

(MA) Macrophage

(N) Neutrophil

(E) Eosinophil

Basophil (B)

(Mc) Mast Cell

[1] Thrombopoietin (TP) [2] Erthropoietin (EP)
[3] Colony Stimulating Factors (C.S.F.)

the Human Immune System

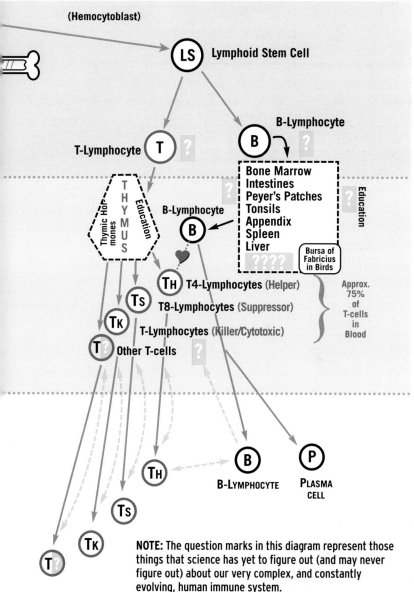

NOTE: The question marks in this diagram represent those things that science has yet to figure out (and may never figure out) about our very complex, and constantly evolving, human immune system.

Some of these fluids that a macrophage excretes tell your body to increase its temperature. This process of increasing the body's temperature is called leukotaxis. It is an amazing process to speed up the rate at which your white blood cells can move through your blood stream and your body. For every degree of temperature rise in your body, the speed at which these white blood cells can travel is doubled. This means that if you have a temperature of 104 degrees, your white blood cells can go 64 times faster than normal to get to the bad guys and kill them or eat them. This proves without a doubt that the age-old process of reducing fevers with drugs goes DIRECTLY AGAINST what your body is doing and INHIBITS AND REDUCES THE ABILITY OF YOUR IMMUNE SYSTEM to heal you.

Other chemicals that the macrophages excrete tell the T-cells and B-cells where and what the deadly invader is. So the macrophages are not only the first cell to get to the invader, kill it and eat it, but they also excrete fluids to help your immune system work faster and also excrete fluid to give information to your T-cells and B-cells, like where the invader is located.

The T-killer cell goes out immediately and kills along with the macrophages. It kills any invader that can hurt you, quick and fast. The T-4 lymphocytes, or T-helper cells, are the communicators. They go out and communicate with the T-lymphocytes, see what's happening and then communicate back to the B-cells what the specific invader is. The B-cells can then, with their surface immunoglobulin, create a poison that is specifically for and specifically lethal to the invader. So the T-helper cells are great communicators. That's why you see a little heart between that cell and the B-cell on my diagram. The T-suppressor cells (T-8 lymphocytes) are also very important—it's their job to detect when the war has been won and then to de-escalate the war, to stop the attack and communicate to the other T-cells and B-cells that your immune system has won. There are many other T-cells and their action is currently being investigated.

The B-cells, the other major type of cell created from your lymphoid stem cell (as I mentioned earlier) have a chemical on their surface called immunoglobulin. There are five known types of immunoglobulin in us. They are IgA, IgD, IgE, IgG and IgM, and the Ig at the beginning simply stands for immunoglobulin.

The B-cells use this immunoglobulin on their surface to create what is called an antibody, which is a specific poison that will kill a specific invader. Antibodies are manufactured by the B-cells with a particular shape designed to fit exactly onto the foreign invader like a key fits a specific lock. The antibody, once attached, destroys the invader.

This is the REAL FLU VACCINE my friends, a specific vaccine, made by your immune system and your body, exactly for the specific bacteria or virus that you have been infected with. Not some dead animal pus and mercury mixed up by a drug company last year guessing which of the thousands, probably millions, of different germs you might be infected with today. I'll take the one my body makes!

If you are interested, re-read this section and when doing so, look at the chart I made. If you do this a few times, it will all begin to make some sense. If it does, you might understand some of the information you hear from either your doctor or the news media about disease and immunity.

If it doesn't, just skip it. You don't need to know any of this to heal yourself and be well.

PREVENTION

CHAPTER 4

9 EFFECTIVE COLD & FLU
PREVENTION TIPS

QUICK REFERENCE CHART

1 Avoid Sick People and Crowds

2 Start Preventative Natural Medicine

3 Clean The Air

4 Wash Your Hands More Often

5 Keep Your Fingers OUT of Your Nose, Mouth and Eyes

6 Keep Warm and Don't Get a Chill

7 Get More Movement and Sun

8 Get Your Eight Hours of Sleep

9 Avoid Negativity

Before we get into any of the Natural Routines, foods, juices and Herbal Medicines to treat colds and influenza, there are also many simple and easy steps you can take to PREVENT getting infected and sick in the first place. **And, if you follow these steps during cold and influenza season, you can greatly reduce and even eliminate the chances of you getting infected.** So, take these steps VERY SERIOUSLY, because by following them you can save yourself a lot of pain, suffering and money. Maybe most important, you will be healthy and strong to nurse your sick family and friends back to health.

Come on, I know you have heard it before from mom or grandma (or someone with some great wisdom) that, **"An ounce of PREVENTION is worth a pound of cure"**. This couldn't be more true than when it comes to preventing colds and flu.

If we know for a fact that we are in the midst of the cold and flu season, a time of the year when we are at a much greater risk of getting infected, then why not take common sense preventative measures that are proven to greatly reduce your risk of getting an infection in the first place? They are so simple and easy, almost too simple and too easy, but also EXTREMELY EFFECTIVE measures that will PROTECT you and PREVENT you from getting infected.

STEP #1: Avoid Sick People And Crowds

This is the most important tip on this whole list. The reason is simply that if you do get infected with a cold or influenza, it will be by another person, or their saliva or bodily fluids. The absolute number one way to avoid infection is simply to avoid infected people. During the cold and flu season, I literally avoid people like the plague. I am a bit of a loner anyway, but during this time of year, I become a bit of a hermit. Now, I certainly understand that most people can't avoid contact with others, and I also understand that you cannot easily tell who is infected and who isn't, and you can't see the infection or the droplets, because they don't light up like the alien blood from *Predator*. This is where all of the additional preventative tips and measures will come in handy, just in case you do come into contact with someone who is infected.

I also understand that some people must eat out in restaurants, where many infected people may be touching the plates, cutlery or even the food, and that many people must travel during the holidays, or during the cold and flu season, so if you must, BE CAREFUL. The first thing I suggest for those *mingling* with the general public in the next segment, "Start Preventative Natural Medicine", is to make sure that you are healthy *before* you eat out, and *before* you travel, and take your herbal medicine with you so you can use it *while you are traveling*. This will have a huge impact on you staying well and infection free.

STEP #2: Start Preventative Natural Medicine

There are two herbal medicines that you can use at the beginning of every month to PROTECT you from getting infected.

First, it is proven that keeping your blood rich with nutrients, keeps your immune and defensive systems at peak operating performance. This is simply because vitamins, minerals, amino acids, enzymes and other nutrients are your body's building blocks that it needs to build all immune cells, immune chemicals, immunoglobulin, interferon, antibodies, and to wage any war against the invaders at a moment's notice. The best way to make sure you have this nutrition in your blood is eating plenty of organic, live, fruits, vegetables, grains, seeds, nuts and sprouts—basically a healthy and vital vegan food program. Also, add in your organic fresh fruit and vegetable juices, which build your blood and your immune system. In addition, top this healthy food program off with my **SuperFood Plus** formula to assure you that you have all the nutrients you need in your blood. A single daily dose will give your body 100% or more of all the vitamins it needs, and only from foods and herbs, not man-made chemicals. This is *recognizable nutrition* for your body that it can assimilate in minutes. I have always told my patients, yes

Echinacea tells your body to build more immune cells and immune chemicals, but what are you going to build them out of? Pizza? Beer? Junk Food? **I don't think so.** So I want to make sure you have all the nutrition you need to build strong and powerful immunity, and **SuperFood Plus** give you that assurance. In addition to all of this, **SuperFood Plus** is rich in natural spirulina beta-carotene Vitamin A and acerola cherry Vitamin-C, both which have natural infection-fighting and immune-stimulating ability.

Second, I always had my patients "tone up" and "tune up" their immune system on a regular basis, every month during cold and influenza season. The best way to do this is by taking one **Cold & Flu Herbal "SHOT"** every day, for the first week of every month, September through April. This simply keeps you ahead of the game, boosting your immune system before any bacterial or viral attack. The best and easiest way to do this is to simply empty one of my **Cold & Flu Herbal "SHOTS"** into a sports bottle (like my Dr. Schulze Sports Bottle with my healing recipes on the side), and then fill it up with you favorite beverage, like fresh organic fruit or vegetable juice. Then, just take this bottle with you, out into the world every day, and just make sure that the bottle is empty by the time you get home in the evening. Do this for six days every month and your immune system will be an impenetrable barrier.

Note: I had one Hollywood patient tell me that they put these two herbal medicines into lite beer and drank it that way every morning. All I can say is that it is a heck of a lot better than just lite beer by itself!

There is nothing more protective and PROACTIVE than a strong defense and a strong offense and these two herbal medicines will do exactly that to protect you.

Finally, I don't want to state the obvious, but it is also very important that you are healthy and don't have any illness or dis-eases before going into cold and flu season. If you do, we are fighting an uphill battle and your immune system is more exhausted than supercharged. So, if you need to, now is the perfect time to do one of my **5-Day Detox Programs**, either for the bowel, the liver or the kidneys; you choose. If in doubt, do the bowel. A nice easy pre-cold and flu season detox is the perfect way to ensure you are strong, healthy and CLEAN going into the cold and flu season.

STEP #3: Clean The Air

If you must be around others, try to keep the air as fresh and clean as possible. Remember, we learned in the chapter "What Are Colds and Influenza?", that most of these types of infections are "droplet born infections" and that we often get infected by coming into contact and inhaling infected saliva and mucous droplets, from the infected persons sneezing or coughing in the same room with us.

One way to make sure the air you are breathing is "droplet-free" is to place an air purifier in your home or office that has an ionizer and a HEPA filter to literally destroy and "filter out" the infected material *before* you inhale it.

An additional way is to spray my **Air Detox** formula liberally throughout the room you are in multiple times a day. The pure essential oils in this formula kill bacteria and virus on contact, which will also prevent you from getting infected.

And if possible, get more fresh air (even if it's cold air) by opening up windows in your home or office more this time of year, to get the infected air out and the pure air in.

Just imagine my clinic during this time of the year, filled with sick people coughing, sneezing and choking. My interns would spray my **Air Detox** formula through the air in my waiting room about every five minutes, and into the air in my office before, after and sometimes even during my consultations to keep me and other patients from getting constantly infected.

You can also wear a surgical mask, or "old-timey" bad guy or cowboy scarf (even Michael Jackson thought this was cool). This may be extreme, but if I have to be around sick, infected people, it's better than breathing their infection.

Also in the winter, artificially-heated rooms don't get fresh air and become dryer with much lower humidity levels. There is new research available which shows that this literally *dehydrates* the water in the infected "droplets" causing them to disperse more in the air and spread more and maybe even stay active longer. I don't know if all of this is true, but it still promotes the idea of getting fresh air into the room. So do like my mother used to do even in the dead cold of winter... get the windows open. When my dad would yell at her and ask what she was doing, she would simply respond, "I am airing out the house."

STEP #4: Wash Your Hands More Often

This time of year, you are coming into contact with more infected bacterial and viral "droplets" than at any other time of the year. In fact, many medical researchers believe that the bacteria and virus in these droplets can stay alive, active and dangerous to you, for up to eight hours; some believe even longer. This means that the person whose "droplets" may infect you could have used the toilet, light switch or door handle, and left the building hours before you even got there. They could be in another country by now!

So, the only way you can protect yourself from this exposure is to wash your hands constantly this time of year, at least every hour, especially when you are out and about. **Washing your hands with soap and water will kill the virus and wash it away, *before* it has a chance to infect you.**

STEP #5: Keep Your Fingers OUT of Your Nose, Mouth and Eyes

Again, just assume that you are constantly coming in contact with infected "droplets" this time of the year, and they are all over your hands. Remember they are microscopic, so basically invisible. On your hands they are harmless and won't hurt you, but if you put your fingers into your nose, eyes or mouth, the bacteria and virus can now easily transfer and enter your upper respiratory tract, and now the infection is in your body. Frequent handwashing is only part one of this safety protocol and preventative practice, but not inserting your fingers into your mucous membrane tissue is part two. If you follow these two steps, you will greatly decrease your chances of getting infected all winter long.

STEP #6: Keep Warm and Don't Get a Chill

Our parents and grandparents knew the validity of this common advice, even though medicine and science always "pooh-poohed" it, saying that there was no scientific evidence that exposing yourself to cold or getting a chill had any effect on you getting a cold. Well, until now. Over the past decade, there have been more and more scientific and medical reports linking the body getting cold, and getting chilled, to effectively lowering your resistance and making you more susceptible to getting a bacterial or viral infection. New studies now show that people who are exposed to cold for longer periods of time have more cold and flu infections than those that are not. Now, I'm not saying that you shouldn't join the Polar Bear Club. Heck, I love jumping into cold streams in the wintertime, and even hopping out of the hot tub onto the fresh snow to make some naked snow angels, then getting my butt back into the hot tub. That's just good, old hydrotherapy! This is a lot different. I am talking about *prolonged* exposure to cold temperatures and getting a chill. So bundle up and stay warm out there. It will keep your immune system strong.

STEP #7: Get More Movement and Sun

Moving your body is not just exercise to have toned muscles, it is much, much more. Every function in your body depends upon your moving—everything—your blood circulation, your lymphatic circulation (which is your IMMUNE SYSTEM) and your nerve function, digestion, assimilation, elimination, your brain—everything.

Your immune system, your lymphatic system, does not have a pump like your blood circulation has your heart. It totally depends on you moving your body to massage and pump your white blood immune cells around your body through your lymphatic system. No movement, no immune system circulation!

Naturally, we all slow down during the winter months, so make sure you are getting some fresh air and moving every day. I want you to sweat, bend and stretch. Yeah, walking, running, bending, stretching, yoga, dancing, sex—whatever. Just do it for an hour every day.

Some of the best movements to stimulate and circulate your lymphatic fluid are yoga and deep breathing, but ANYTHING you do that is fun is the best. Remember, when it comes to exercise and moving, FUN is FUNdamental.

Even in the winter, if it is sunny, get out and catch some rays. New research shows that low Vitamin D levels are closely associated with an increased risk of getting cold and flu infections. And, the best way to boost up your Vitamin D is simply to get outside for 10 or 15 minutes a day. The old European Naturopathic doctors and "Nature Cure" doctors, the lineage of my great teachers, believed whole-heartedly in sun and air baths, even in the dead of winter, getting outside naked, for at least 10 minutes a day. I have never needed much of an excuse to drop my clothing, even in the winter, so now I have yet another reason.

STEP #8: Get Your Eight Hours of Sleep

Many studies have now concluded that lack of sleep (less than seven or eight hours) can double your chances of getting a bacterial or viral infection when exposed to it, compared to people who get the proper amount of sleep on a regular basis. Other studies have shown it to be much higher, like three to ten times more. The bottom line is that we know that getting a consistent eight hours of sleep each night is one of the absolute keys to longevity, and now it seems that it is also a key to keeping a strong and powerful immune system that will better protect you from infection.

STEP #9: Avoid Negativity

Nothing depresses your immune system more effectively and more quickly than negative people. So, literally avoid them, like the plague. In fact, the same way I started out this section, by telling you to avoid sick, infected and physically ill people, I also suggest you avoid and stay clear of the *emotionally* unwell.

Negative people, angry people, argumentative people, dysfunctional people, emotionally and spiritually unwell people will give a negative blast to your immune system as effectively as junk food, sugar and tobacco. So, stay clear.

I would also avoid any concentrated negative input like the television news that rolls up all the most horribly, horrifying and worst things that happened on the planet today and spews it back to you in a 30-minute immune destroying blast. I prefer to know that 99.9999999% of the people on this planet had a pretty great day today. It was only one loser that had their arm torn off by a crocodile, and I don't want to know about that!

The Bottom Line

Look, even according to the Center for Disease Control's website on Swine Flu, they suggest that in order to have a strong capable immune system, that you stay in good general health by getting plenty of sleep, being physically active, managing your stress, drinking plenty of fluids and eating nutritious food. YES! I couldn't have said it better myself—sounds like they have been visiting the Dr. Schulze website and following my guidelines to Creating Powerful Health.

CHAPTER 5
WHAT TO DO AT THE FIRST SIGN OF A COLD OR FLU

Many interviewers have asked me over the years, why is it that I have had so much success with my patients and customers having miraculous healing results from degenerative diseases like cancer, heart disease, neurological diseases, even AIDS, and I have thought about this at length. The answer is actually quite simple; it's intensity. I just turned up the dial higher.

Most doctors, especially in the Natural Healing world (and, believe it or not, in the medical world too) are afraid of hurting their patients. After all, their motto is "do no harm". On the other hand, **my motto is "Get Well NOW!"**

It is important to understand right in the beginning that most of my patients, especially in the last decade of my extremely busy clinical practice, and also because they had wasted lots of time messing around with medical doctors, that by the time they got an appointment to see me, I would say on the average, **it was four months AFTER their medical doctor said they would be dead.** In fact, we often joked about them as being the *walking dead*. So I, and they, really had nothing to lose. They were already supposed to be dead. So I was NOT going to pussyfoot around with them when it came to the intensity of my programs or the dosages of my herbal medicines. After all, looking back, the only ones who died were the ones who did not do enough, did not take enough or wimped out, not the ones who did too much. **Consequently, I tried to literally drown them with wheatgrass juice, turn them inside out with flushing and detoxification routines and kill them with supposedly "dangerous" and "irresponsible" dosages** of my extra-potent herbal medicines, and all that ended up happening was… they got well.

My patients taught me two very important things… One, that intensive aggressive natural treatment turns supposedly killer diseases around and makes them go away. And two, when in doubt, do more and take more!

Before I tell you what to do, to be clear, in my clinic my nickname was "Adolph Schulze". I was a tough Natural Healing, ass-kicking Gestapo looking for highly dedicated and tough stormtroopers that were ready to take on ANY disease and illness, kick ass and take names. I was Attila the Hun, Genghis Khan, General George Patton or Lt. Aldo Raine from *Inglourious Basterds***… Whatever your vision is of a ruthless butt-kicking son of a bitch, that was me. The words "defeat" or "lose" just were not in my vocabulary. I pushed my patients further than they could ever imagine doing themselves. That was my job. SO REMEMBER THIS, when you are wondering anywhere in this book if I meant what I said, or that you should take another dose, a bigger dose or exceed any of my instructions, the answer is YES, YES, YES and YES!**

OK, One Last Story…

I spent my life studying the Martial Arts, earning three Black Belts amongst many other certifications. I fought full contact and kickboxed for years and towards the end of my career, in my quest for the ultimate fighting techniques, I found myself in the early 1980s enrolled in the Filipino Kali Academy in Torrance, California, studying with Bruce Lee's protégé, Guro Danny Inosanto and Richard Bustillo. Today, one of *their* top students, and I am proud to say a friend of mine, is Master Paul Vunak. Master Vunak, with his Progressive Fighting Systems, teaches the elite of the elite, from Navy Seals to numerous clandestine government agencies, simply how to kill. I have had the honor of training with Master Vunak and even taught with him, and just one of his many techniques he calls the RAT, which stands for Rapid Assault Tactics. I love this technique, as he describes it, it is a system of "getting in and getting out fast". It is extremely physical, even barbaric, and the number one focus is to SURVIVE. He took the words right out of my mouth! I couldn't have said it better, and this is exactly my focus at the first signs of a cold or flu.

▸ **Get IN FAST!**

▸ **Be EXTREMELY and INTENSELY PHYSICAL!**

▸ **The FOCUS is to SURVIVE!**

I am proud to say that Master Vunak is also a follower of my work, uses my herbal medicines and has even asked me to speak at his seminar. I always say if a philosophy is true and good, then it will apply to everything, from love and peace to war and conflict, from family to business and from killing to healing.

Remember my friends, medical doctors do not mess around. If you are sick they will be so aggressive that they often kill people attempting to heal them—in fact, they kill millions. I just match their level of intensity and aggression, but in a completely natural and holistic way.

OK, Now What To Do...

You know what it feels like, you wake up in the morning, or come home from work and all of a sudden you have that "uh-oh" feeling. For everyone this feeling is a little different. It can be that you notice you are a bit sweaty, in the face, cheeks or forehead, and feel a slight bit feverish. For others, it is a scratchy soreness or burning in the throat, while for others it is sneezing, or a runny nose or a cough and some lung congestion. For others, the first thing they notice is feeling body aches (often in the lower back) or a headache. So, two very important things right here:

#1: Trust Your INSTINCT! If you think you are sick, you are!

#2: Get Real AGGRESSIVE! Rapid assault tactics, right now!

Whatever your initial symptoms are, you have been infected with a cold or flu, and it is now well documented that initial aggressive treatment does many things.

First, if caught early enough, **you can actually STOP a cold or flu dead in its tracks.** What I mean by that is that a rapid aggressive response can often stop an infection, before it knows what happened and has a chance to literally "divide and conquer" more in your body. Bacteria and viruses multiply and take over your cells and your body; they literally eat you. But, if they can be killed in their very early stages, well, you can defeat them before you get a full-blown infection.

Second, there is no downside to this aggressive response, because studies also prove that even if the infection gets established in you, that **early aggressive treatment will reduce symptoms by up to 50% or more and also reduce the duration of the infection by 50% or more**. So, the worst-case scenario to aggressive treatment, even if you do get infected, **is half the pain and half the time**, in other words **half the cold or flu.** This means you have nothing to lose and everything to gain by being an aggressive animal. Sometimes you have to kick some ass, and NOW IS THAT TIME!

The Importance of "AGGRESSIVE Purification"

Once you have had contact with the bacteria or virus, the micro-organisms start multiplying in your body very soon, often only after a few hours. You can start to feel the symptoms in as little as 8 to 12 hours, but it usually takes a few days for you to notice you have been infected.

This is why it is so important to be VERY AGGRESSIVE at the first moment that you get what I call that "uh-oh" feeling, when you know that something is up and you have been infected. Because in those very first hours that you notice you are infected, **you may have actually been infected for days**, at least for hours, and the quicker you can start the natural defensive health and immune building and the natural offensive attack against these alien microbes, the better. That way you have a chance at kicking its ass before it kicks yours.

Over the years in the clinic, thousands of my patients have been able to defeat colds and influenza within hours with an extremely aggressive natural counter attack, and even though many medical doctors claim this is impossible, it is not! (Well, actually it is impossible if you're using medical methods and injecting or ingesting poison.)

TREATMENT

CHAPTER 6

10 STEPS OF AGGRESSIVE PURIFICATION FOR COLDS AND INFLUENZA

QUICK REFERENCE CHART

1 STOP Eating Immediately

2 START Drinking Immediately

3 Take a HEROIC DOSE of Herbal Medicine

4 PREPARE Yourself and Your House

5 Cold & Flu "Busting" Hydrotherapy BATH

6 Take Another Cold & Flu Herbal "SHOT"

7 PREPARE Your Bedroom

8 Stay POSITIVE

9 Make Sure You Are CLEAN Inside

10 Make My Potassium Broth

STEP #1: STOP Eating Immediately!

One of the first things to do is to STOP eating. There have been many old-time anecdotes about "feed a cold and starve a fever", or is it the other way around? What did grandma say? Well, it doesn't matter, because it is simply STARVE EVERYTHING. The best way to prepare to wage war is to STOP all food intake until you are feeling strong, healthy and in the clear.

It takes a lot of blood and a lot of your body's energy to process, digest, assimilate and eliminate food. And instead, all of this blood and energy can be utilized by your body and immune system, to put up its strongest defense and counter attack.

So IMMEDIATELY get out the juicer and start juicing, and stay on pure water, herbal teas and fresh organic fruit and vegetable juice until you are well, even a for few days after. And, drink plenty of them. Drink at least one gallon a day of liquids until you are well. Flush yourself real good!

Almost everyone will notice that when they are infected with a cold or flu, or have any illness or dis-ease, they are not hungry anyway. This is your body telling you to fast. I am just asking you to do what your body is trying to communicate to you naturally, and putting it into words. STOP EATING FOOD!

STEP #2: START Drinking Immediately!

Consuming more liquids is a very important part of naturally treating colds and flu. Come on, even medical doctors suggest to get more bed rest and **drink more fluids** when you have a cold or flu. Getting more fluids in your body gives you the building blocks for more immune cells and immune chemicals. It is also important to stay very hydrated, especially if you have a fever.

So I want you to drink a big glass, at least 16 ounces (if not a quart) of water and fresh organic fruit juice.

A great drink is to simply take a quart of purified water and heat it up (warm to hot, but not so hot that you can't drink it right away).

Then, squeeze the juice of 1 or 2 lemons and 1 lime into it, or any citrus combination. Then, I would add a small pinch of cayenne pepper or a few drops of **Cayenne Tincture**, but don't make it so spicy and hot that you won't drink it. Finally, juice a piece of fresh ginger root (about the size of your thumb) and add the juice into this drink also.

Sometimes, I even add one of my **Cold & Flu Herbal "SHOTS"** right into this drink, or I just follow the next step, Step #3. If you are feeling really infected, do both!

STEP #3: Take A HEROIC DOSE Of Herbal Medicine!

What I mean by "heroic" is to simply take a very large dose. As I look back at my decades of clinical practice and I see the mistakes patients made, it was always not doing enough and not taking enough, but NEVER doing too much. The worst thing I ever saw from people seriously overdosing on my herbal medicine or my Natural Healing routines was a good vomit. On the other hand, many died or got worse before they got better and suffered needlessly, because they didn't do enough. I learned that the far bigger downside is to error on not doing enough.

So, I STRONGLY suggest at the first sign of any infection, especially a cold or flu, to start taking large doses of the juices, foods and herbs that we know will heal you. This is why I designed this first herbal medicine...

Cold & Flu Herbal "SHOT"

Normally, people will take a few droppersful of an herbal tonic, and normally this is OK. But nowhere in this book am I talking normal. I am talking about an infection that could take your life, so let's throw the word normal out.

The medicinal use of the Echinacea herb goes back to the American Indians. It is a powerful immune system stimulant, causing your body to increase both its immune cells and immune chemicals. Many herbal doctors believe if you take too much, you could "burn out" your immune system. I have NEVER seen this happen and I have used larger doses of the most powerful Echinacea tonics for longer durations than anybody. But again, my clinic and treatment was much more like an emergency room trauma center so the dosages I talk about and suggest in this manual may seem extreme for some people. Having said that…

At the first sign of any cold or flu infection, I used to beg my patients to take a huge dose, 12 droppersful of my **Echinacea Plus** to immediately shock their immune system into high gear, along with 6 droppersful of my **SuperTonic**, which will kill any bacteria, virus, fungus, anything, on contact. I used to tell them to mix this in one or two ounces of juice, and on and on, and after years of this begging, my son said to me, "Why don't you just make this drink for them?" So I did. I called it my **Cold & Flu Herbal "SHOT"**. The first part of this formula is 12 droppersful of my **Echinacea Plus,** which contains Echinacea root blends, Echinacea seeds, Habanero peppers (to make the Echinacea work much faster and stronger) and Garlic (to kill all harmful pathogens). I also added 6 droppersful of my **SuperTonic**, which contains Garlic bulb, Onion bulb, Horseradish root, Habanero peppers and Hawaiian Yellow Ginger rhizome. This formula kills any pathogen on contact. To this I add enough organic Acerola cherry to give you an assailable blast of natural Vitamin-C (actually 1,000%—10 times—your RDI!) Then, I add a dozen more herbs that I used in the clinic that are powerfully effective for the sinus, tonsils, lungs, fevers, etc.

So, at the first sign of that "uh-oh" feeling, I want you to take one of my **Cold & Flu Herbal "SHOTS"** IMMEDIATELY! You should shake it to mix up the contents from any settling and to get any of the thicker ingredients off of the bottom of the bottle. Take about half of the bottle's contents into your mouth and gargle for at least 30 seconds, covering your tonsils and then swallow the contents. Then, immediately do this again, using the second half of the bottle. You should have at least one six-pack of these in your kitchen or bathroom cupboard during cold and

flu season just because if you get infected, you will not have time
to order it, and then wait days for the delivery. Worse, sometimes
during the worst influenza outbreaks, the roads are also snowed
and iced in and the delivery trucks can't get to your house. So have
a box in your house, because when you need it, you need to get it
in you immediately!

SuperFood Plus

I already discussed the importance of getting your blood flooded
with nutrition to effectively fight off infection, but if you need
another herbal nudge, go back and read it again under "9 Effective
Cold & Flu Prevention Tips".

But now that we know that you are infected, I want you to take
a DOUBLE dose of **SuperFood Plus**, so you can build the most
powerful immune system and most lethal immune response.

I find that when you are already drinking so much liquid, that last
thing you want is another 16-ounce **SuperFood Plus** drink, so this
is where the **SuperFood Plus** tablets come in real handy. I would
just start taking them and don't stop until you have swallowed 30
tablets (that's a double dosage). Don't rush—you can take a few
hours to do this.

Raw Garlic

At the end of this book, under "General Information", the first
section is on one herb, GARLIC. This is simply because you
cannot find a stronger and more effective broad-spectrum antibiotic, anti-viral, anti-fungal cold and flu, bacterial and viral
destroying super herb, PERIOD. If you need more stimulus, go
read that chapter now.

Now my **Echinacea Plus** contains garlic, and my **SuperTonic**
contains garlic, and both of these formula are in my **Cold & Flu
Herbal "SHOT"**, you guessed it, along with ADDITIONAL

garlic, but I still want you to get more in. So get chopping and consume some raw garlic now, at least three cloves, just chop it and swallow it if necessary, but just get it down.

STEP #4: PREPARE!

PREPARE Yourself
It is also a good idea to prepare yourself mentally for an aggressive Natural Healing program over the next few days, so you might need to call in for a day off work and/or cancel a few appointments or plans, at least modify your schedule. If you need to tell anyone anything, simply tell them that you have been infected, and are going to do some aggressive purification and Natural Healing, Dr. Schulze style. Basically, we are going to kick this microbe's ass, not the other way around (a positive outlook is extremely important for a powerful immunity, see Chapter 3 on your immune system). Remember, you are what you think!

PREPARE Your House
Now is a great time to take a small visual check and inventory. Make sure you have the water, herbal teas, fresh fruit and vegetables to juice, or the juice itself, the herbal medicines, garlic, ginger and everything else you need to launch and maintain your aggressive purification.

If you are missing anything, it may be time to call in a favor. Call a friend, relative or someone you live with and give them a list of your needs—but, get what you need in your kitchen and into your house. For a list of supplies that you will need to do this "10-Step Aggesive Purification", see Chapter 11 on page 103.

STEP #5: My Cold & Flu "Busting" Hydrotherapy Bath Routine!
Hydrotherapy is basically just a fancy name for a water therapy routine to detoxify and cleanse the body. This specific hydrotherapy treatment is one that I designed and refined in my clinic. It is now famous for its ability to stop a cold or influenza infection dead in its tracks.

Baths such as this have been used for thousands of years, in every culture on the planet. They were also very popular healing routines in the 1700s and 1800s and even in the first half of the 1900s, in health spas and hydrotherapy clinics worldwide, until the popular use of aspirin and antibiotics came into fashion.

My teachers and their teachers before them had many methods. From the treatments of Vincenz Priessnitz and the herbal hydrotherapy of Father Sebastian Kneipp to Benedict Lust and his famous "Blood Washing Method" to Dr. John Ray Christopher's "Cold Sheet Treatment", I have seen hundreds of different hydrotherapy treatments. I have also traveled all over the world visiting hydrotherapy spas and treatment centers that still exist today to take their "cures". And, I have also administered hundreds of hydrotherapy treatments to my patients over the years.

I have seen many specific hydrotherapy treatments for specific diseases and I have personally witnessed them create almost instant healing miracles. From paralysis to chronic depression, I have seen the miracles.

The following routine is one that I developed *specifically* for treating people with cold and influenza infections. And if done IMMEDIATELY, it can end an infection *before* it spreads any further in your body.

I suggest doing this hydrotherapy routine for the first two evenings at the first sign of cold or influenza infections.

My Cold & Flu "Busting" Hydrotherapy Routine has many actions on your body. First, this routine is diaphoretic, which means it will make you sweat, and sweat profusely. This will help to detoxify and purify your body.

Next, this routine will increase your body's temperature. Remember, a fever is your friend, as long as you stay hydrated. For every degree of temperature rise in your body, the speed at which your bacterial and viral fighting white blood cells can travel IS DOUBLED! So, let's get hot and sweaty! More accurately, let's amp up and stimulate your immune system into high gear.

So here is how to do it—it takes a little preparation, and a little focus at first, but like most things, once you do it one time, you will know how to do it and it is really easy...

NOTE & CAUTION: If you are on your own, I highly suggest just doing my Standard Routine, which is the main routine suggested. If you have a supportive friend or partner, and you have done the Standard Routine at least once, and you are more seriously ill or just want to have a Natural Healing adventure, then you can choose the more healing and more intense options that I have highlighted in a few sections. Since there is the possibility of becoming faint during this routine, always have your Cayenne Tincture available and handy during this entire hydrotherapy routine, to keep you alert and very conscious.

FIRST: Turn the heater on in your bathroom and get the room as hot as you possibly can, like a sauna. If you don't have a separate heater in your bathroom, get a small portable space heater **but keep it far away from the bathtub.** Water and electricity do not play well together. For this reason, always make sure that any heating appliance in your bathroom is plugged into a special Ground Fault Interruption (GFI) electrical outlet for safety. NOW, GET YOUR BATHROOM VERY HOT!

SECOND: Prepare some hot tea. Peppermint, ginger, it doesn't have to be anything fancy, you can just grate some fresh ginger root and throw a handful of peppermint leaves into a pot of boiling water, squeeze a lemon or lime in, a pinch of cayenne pepper or a few drops of **Cayenne Tincture**, and make it hot, but not too hot, so you can drink it, not sip it, and drink it rapidly. I like just hot **Detox Tea**, so if you have that around, just boil some up. I want you to drink at least two 8-ounce cups of this, and try to drink four 8-ounce cups of it, or 1-quart, while you are in the tub. So, get your tea prepared and ready.

NOTE, if you are constipated, now is the time to give yourself a high enema, before you even start this routine.

THIRD: Fill your bathtub with hot water, about as hot as you can stand it. Spray 10 to 12 pumps of **Air Detox** into the air, saturate the air with this formula and continue to spray it in the air during this entire routine.

NOTE: THE FOLLOWING IS NOT NECESSARY. I do not suggest it if this is your first time doing this bath, or if you don't have a friend to help you while doing this program.

Having said that, if you want to increase the intensity and effectiveness of this bath, add some cayenne powder, ginger root powder and mustard powder (equal parts) into this bath. A handful of each will do. Just place the herbal powders into a tea towel or cotton cloth and then tie it with a string or rope, so the herbs don't leak out. Then place this giant "tea bag" into the tub and soak it and squeeze it a number of times, and the water in the tub will turn a nice orange color.

If you do this, you MUST coat your genitals, anus and any other sensitive areas of your body with a protective ointment. Many people use Vaseline, which is disgusting, toxic petroleum jelly, but it works. I prefer natural ointments, but whatever you use, PUT A LOT ON, as you do not want your genitals to be on fire. Bottom line, I would rather use Vaseline than have an intensely burning penis or vagina.

This hydrotherapy bath can be intense, and I always suggest having a friend around when doing it. If you add the herbs to the bath, the helper should coax you to stay in the bath even after you are crying and want to get out.

You will see the bathwater changing color and smell the aroma of the herbs. Sometimes the aroma can make you cough. GREAT!

FOURTH: Bring one-quart of hot tea into the bathroom and put it right next to the tub, so you can reach it and drink it while you are in the tub.

FIFTH: Get into the bath, relax, sink down and get the hot water all over you. Now, start drinking your hot tea. You must consume all of it while you are in the bath, probably in the next 15 minutes, because you are going to get hot and want to get out of the bath. Also, while you are in the bath, keep squeezing the herbs in the bath if you did this part.

CAUTION: It is possible to feel a little faint when doing this routine. If possible, you should always have a friend around when doing this routine to give you a cold slap with a washcloth or a dose of **Cayenne Tincture** right in your mouth while you are in the hot tub. Most people need this and get a bit weak and maybe even dizzy, so a healing "buddy" is always a great idea.

SIXTH: Add more hot water into the bath while you are in the tub and do not let the water cool down. In fact, make it even hotter while you are in the tub. Make the bath as hot as you can stand it. Also, force yourself to drink all of the tea. The bath should take 30 minutes.

If you also put the herbs into the bath, it is even possible that you might feel a strong tingling, maybe even a little burning in your most sensitive areas. This is normal. Maybe some of you will feel a lot of burning, depending on how much herbs you put into the bath.

SEVENTH: Once you are done with the bath, get out (be careful as you may be weak and dizzy) and get into the shower. Now, I would like you to do my **7 Repetitions Hot and Cold Alternating Shower...**

Hot water sedates you, relaxes you, and while it's relaxing you, it loosens your muscles. It also brings all the blood in your body to the very surface, which is why your skin turns red.

Cold water does just the opposite—it stimulates you, it wakes you up. It contracts the muscles and it drives all the blood that's on the surface of your body into the deeper organs.

By alternating from hot to cold and then back to hot again, you are bringing the blood to the surface of your body, then driving it back to the center core of your body, and then drawing your blood back to the surface again.

This is much more powerful and much faster at moving your blood and lymphatic fluid than any massage, exercise or even the hottest cayenne pepper. Now, just imagine if you did them all!

Just get into a nice warm shower (a blend of hot and cold water) for a few minutes and relax. When you're ready, quickly turn the hot water off all the way, and take that full blast of cold water on your entire body, everywhere, especially the sick areas, not forgetting your head. It is also helpful to scream, yell, moan, cry, shake and do whatever comes naturally. Actually, what usually comes naturally is very little because we have had years of training in swallowing our emotional expression, so unload and scream.

After about 15-30 seconds (whatever you can stand) turn the hot water back up slowly, and then take a few seconds, and turn it up as hot as you can stand it. Make sure that it hits you everywhere again for about 15 seconds, even up to a minute if you can. Then, immediately turn the hot water off all the way.

If you understood me correctly, you will be turning the hot water on and off, but you will be leaving the cold water running.

Once you get the hang of this, I want you to do seven repetitions of hot and cold, that is seven "hots" and seven "colds".

NOTE: If you have a history of heart or circulatory disease, work your way into this program slowly, using common sense.

EIGHTH: After the shower, finish with hot water for at least two minutes, and then dry off and put on some sweat clothes (natural fibers of course) and get into bed. Cover up with a few blankets and keep the heat and sweating going. Next to the bed, you should have all of your additional herbal medicines, water, juices, more herbal tea and whatever else you need so you can now stay in bed overnight.

NOTE: For those patients that are critically ill, I suggest using a cold wet sheet here. Simply have a cotton sheet soaking in ice water, next to the shower, and cover the mattress or futon in your bed with some protective sheeting on it, like plastic. Then, when you are done with the **7 Repetitions Hot and Cold Alternating Shower**, wrap the cold icy sheet all around your body and get right into bed, and cover up with a few blankets. **If you prefer, you can use a sweatshirt and sweatpants, this makes it a little easier and more effective, and have them soaking in the ice water instead of the cotton sheet.** The icy cold sheet or sweat clothes will cause your body to superheat up, to dispel the cold. I used this same routine in my clinic as part of my "Incurables Program" for my patients with cancer and other supposedly incurable diseases, and watched the miracles happen.

FINAL: In the morning, you will awake refreshed, revitalized and probably healed. Take a cool shower and clean off. If you are not feeling totally healed yet, make this day an Aggressive Purification Day and spend all of your energy healing yourself. Then, in the evening, do my Cold & Flu Busting Hydrotherapy Bath again, this time with even more gusto, and maybe with the more intensive options!

STEP #6: Take Another Cold & Flu Herbal "SHOT"!
After the **Hot and Cold Alternating Shower**, and as you are getting into bed, gargle and swallow another **Cold & Flu Herbal "SHOT"** as described in Step #3.

STEP #7: Prepare Your Bedroom!

Now make sure your bedroom is ready for you to get some rest. You should have all the water, herbal teas and fresh juices you need right near your bed, so you don't have to get out of bed to consume them. You should have your **Air Detox** there also, and spray it around your bedroom, bed and pillow (remember it can stain, it is herbal oils). Have a few extra blankets around as you may cool off a bit after you fall asleep, and I want you to stay warm. And, if the weather is not too horrible, I want you to crack a window open so you get some fresh air, even if the air is cold.

Remember, REST is a major healer to assist your body to do its fighting.

STEP #8: Stay POSITIVE!

I told you in Chapter 3 on the immune system that, "You Are What You Think" and that, "Your Immune System is *Listening* and *Reacting* to your Emotional Dialog!" So, instead of depressing yourself with the idea that you are infected, I want you to get powerfully positive with the focus of aggressive purification. No matter how you do it, there is one great truism that I learned in my clinic, and that is that "NOTHING POSITIVE ever comes from BEING NEGATIVE"! So get POSITIVE. Being POSITIVE is a turbo-charger to your immune system. It turns on all of your survival, self-healing and self-repairing mechanisms, making you stronger and healthier.

We also know that being NEGATIVE causes all types of diseases, from high blood pressure and arterial damage to neurological diseases and cancer. But it seems there is absolutely no downside to being POSITIVE!

So, if you get infected, look on the bright side. First, we know that this is how your immune system self-educates itself, and this is a very important part of living a long and healthy life. Also, your body never just does what is needed—it always does a lot more. So, it will heal this infection, and in the process, heal a lot more.

Who knows what precursors to what diseases were lurking in your body? Now, with this infection, your body's immune response and your aggressive purification routines on top of all of this, you are going to do some amazing scrubbing, cleansing, detoxification and healing and truly Create Powerful Health. As far as you know, this is the biggest blessing from God in your lifetime and you are eating up diseases that you didn't even know you had, and that no test available can detect in such microscopic and pre-clinical stages. Be thankful!

I am a master at positive thinking, and can come up with 1,001 reasons why your infection is an absolute blessing, reminding you that this is not a bump in the road of life, but a jewel. However, this is your job to get positive... so get creative.

Oh yes, and once again I'll remind you that, **"Your Immune System is LISTENING and REACTING to your Emotional Dialog!"**

STEP #9: Make Sure You Are Clean Inside!

Remember, I am assuming that you are healthy, and if you are not, you may consider a few of the following.

First, if your bowel has not been working well (and I mean if you have not been having regular, frequent and normal bowel movements every day) then I would also use an enema, and get all of the accumulated waste and toxic poison out of your body. It will be a lot easier for your body to heal itself if it isn't filled with poison, so give yourself a high enema.

If you are not sure what regular, frequent and normal bowel movements are, then give yourself a high enema—and tomorrow during your rest, read my book on my **5-Day BOWEL Detox**.

And, if you have no idea what a high enema is, and are too weak to learn and do it now, then also take one of my **Bowel Flush "SHOTS"** so you will flush out the entire contents of your bowel tomorrow morning.

Even if your bowel is working OK, you still might consider using a few capsules of my **Intestinal Formula #1**, or any of my other intestinal cleansing formulas to help you flush out any accumulated waste and toxins.

STEP #10: Make Some Potassium Broth!

This is a classic "Potato Peeling" Potassium or Healing Broth that has been used by grandmothers and Nature Cure doctors (is there a difference?) for a millennium.

It is basically a vegan (non-chicken) soup. Although chicken soup has received a reputation for being helpful during colds and influenza, it is the other ingredients, and not the chicken, that are helpful. Chicken has the highest bacteria plate count of ANY animal food. Because of this it is the secret weapon of professionals to "cure" septic tank problems, which are almost always caused by people using bleach and killing off the natural bacteria in the septic tank that is necessary for the natural chemical breakdown of the waste. So throw a chicken into the septic tank, and because they are so loaded with bacteria, they get the sewage active again, but you do NOT want this bacterial nightmare in your body! You have enough bacteria or virus now with your cold or flu, so leave the chicken out.

This type of "Potato Peeling" broth was used by ALL of my nature cure doctor teachers, in their clinics, for extra power when cleansing and fasting and doing any detoxification routine. I modified it to my own "recipe" years ago in my clinic.

The vegetables are powerfully alkalinizing to your body, which assists your body to eliminate mucous, acids, waste, toxins and poisons. It is a natural mineral *flush* for your blood and body. It also has enough garlic and onions to cure the Black Plague.

Once you've made it, you can sip it warm for a few days. Always refrigerate the broth overnight and warm it up again the next day.

After two days, you should have consumed it all. If not, toss any left over away and make a new batch on the third day.

This should taste great, and if it doesn't, add some of your own veggie ideas. Enjoy!

Potassium Broth Recipe

Fill a large pot up to a few inches below the top with:

▸ 25% Potato Peels

▸ 25% Chopped Whole Beets and Carrots

▸ 25% Garlic and White Onions

▸ 25% Dark Greens (beet greens, kale, collard, spinach, etc.)

(Note: Purchase beets with the leaves and stems attached and use the leaves and stems for part of your dark greens.)

1. Add a few hot peppers to taste.

2. Add enough distilled water to just cover vegetables and simmer on very low temperature for one to four hours. Do not boil.

3. Strain and drink only the broth.

4. Make enough for two days, and refrigerate the leftover broth the first night.

5. Use only ORGANIC vegetables! We do not want to consume any toxic, immune suppressive insecticides, pesticides or inorganic chemical fertilizers. That is what we are flushing OUT of the body.

Bonus Step

Have any additional Herbal Medicine you may need available.
This may include, but is not limited to:

▸ Extra Cold & Flu Herbal "SHOTS", you will need more!

▸ Echinacea Plus, in case you want to do it "Old School".

▸ SuperTonic, my patients called it "The cure for the common cold"!

▸ Throat & Tonsil Spray, to use right on your infection!

▸ Lung Tonic, to open your air passages and bronchial tubes!

▸ Air Detox, to kill any airborne bacteria and virus and make it easier to breathe!

▸ Deep Tissue Ointment or Oil, to use as an extremely powerful lung and sinus decongesting chest rub!

CHAPTER 7
TREATING FEVERS

> ## QUICK REFERENCE CHART
>
> **❶ Start Drinking More Fluids**
> **(Water, Herbal Tea, Fresh Fruit & Vegetable Juice)**
>
> **❷ Take a Cold & Flu Herbal "SHOT"**
>
> **❸ Take a Cold & Flu "Busting" Hydrotherapy Bath**

A fever is one of the most misunderstood reactions of the human body. It is so misunderstood that most medical doctors I talk to are totally ignorant of the function of a fever. They have been so brainwashed by the pharmaceutical companies (their sales managers) and by their patients demanding antibiotics, that many doctors and patients alike now think that a fever is a *bad thing*. We will need generations of enlightenment and illumination on this subject to break this ignorance doctors and patients alike have fallen into.

Having said that, let me try to shed some light on this wonderful life-saving and most natural and extremely important immune response...

A fever is simply your body's natural response to being infected.

Often the first sign of infection is when one or more of your immune cells that are constantly circulating in your body, maintaining a security patrol, come into contact with a bacteria or virus. This cell may be a Macrophage or even a T-cell, but when it contacts the invading pathogen, it ruthlessly kills it, immediately. You even have immune cells whose job it is to just communicate the information about this attack, and the attacker, back to the reserves and reinforcements to get them more educated and even to the front lines of the battle. Just one of the ways these cells assist in getting more immune cells to the site of the initial infection is by excreting chemicals that heat up the body, and the reason for this is simply, when the body is hotter, the immune cells can travel faster, and get to the pathogen and kill it faster!

Basically your immune cells, like macrophages, excrete immune chemicals, like interleukon, which cause your body to get warmer, so your immune cells can move quicker.

In fact, for every degree that your temperature rises in your body, the speed at which your white blood cells can travel to find and kill the infection, bacteria, virus, cold or flu, is DOUBLED. This process is called *leukotaxis*. So, if you are running a 104-degree fever, this means that your immune cells are speeding through your body at a rate 64 TIMES FASTER than normal.

This proves without a doubt that the age-old process of reducing fevers with drugs goes DIRECTLY AGAINST what your body is doing and INHIBITS AND REDUCES THE ABILITY OF YOUR IMMUNE SYSTEM to heal you!

I can't think of anything worse for you to do at this point than to reduce your fever, which will do the EXACT OPPOSITE of what your body and immune system are trying to accomplish. The bacteria, the virus and the drug companies will love you, but your healing will be slowed down, if not stopped.

The ONLY danger of a fever is if you let yourself become dehydrated, so back to Step #2 (START DRINKING) in the previous chapter, and FLOOD YOURSELF with pure water, herbal teas and fresh organic fruit and vegetable juices.

Also, a classic *old-timey* way that our grandparents dealt with fevers was to assist them, and what they didn't scientifically know was they were actually doing just that. They would suggest to heat the body up to manufacture a fever, or "bring on a sweat" or to induce or even increase a fever, which assists the body in doing the job it wants to do. People all over the world have used saunas, steam baths, sweat lodges or simply a bath tub doing my Cold & Flu Busting Hot Bath Routine, which could be also called my Fever Busting Routine! (See Step #5 of the previous chapter.)

I think the main thing to remember here, my friends, is that if your body has a response to something, it is AWESOME, and we want to ASSIST your body in its healing process, not judge it and definitely NEVER GO AGAINST IT! One of my most favorite and frequent responses to my patients' descriptions of what they were experiencing on my programs was simply "WONDERFUL". Whether they were telling me about a high fever or green worms crawling out of their ears (just kidding, but not really). What I mean is that WHATEVER you experience during a cleanse, detoxification or even a Cold & Flu Aggressive Purification Program, is GREAT, is GOOD, is WONDERFUL. After all, who am I to judge what the body is doing and/or trying to accomplish. Again, my job as a natural doctor is simply to do everything in my power to get the patient to take really, really great care of themselves and to get really healthy. What the body decides to do in this process, well, who am I to judge this? Or worse, get in the way! This is what medical doctors do, not me.

So… your fever is just part your body's healing immune response to being infected.

In recent years, a disease branded as Reye's Syndrome (a type of Toxic Shock Syndrome) has killed many children. Actually, they were killed by the medical doctors' ignorance that I spoke about earlier, and the drug companies' poison. It was discovered that children who had the flu and were then given Aspirin to try to *control* or *reduce* their fevers, fell into rapidly progressing stages of coma and died. No one wants to point any fingers, which is the usual practice with medical doctors and drug companies (not wanting to bite the hand that feeds them), but it is ridiculously obvious that one should not try to *reduce* or *control* a fever unless you are trying to slow down the immune system and help the bacteria or virus to win. So when medical doctors used Aspirin to reduce fevers in children, they killed them. The ignorance continues as now drug companies and medical doctors alike warn not to try to reduce fevers with children using Aspirin, now they say to use *Acetaminophen instead!*

Some of the best ways to ASSIST a fever to do its job and to ASSIST your immune system are:

STEP #1
Drinking More Fluids: Staying hydrated allows your body to get as hot as it needs to enhance your immune ability.

STEP #2
Cold & Flu Herbal "SHOT": Among many other things, it has diaphoretic herbs in it, which promote sweating. This greatly ASSISTS the fever and your body's immune stimulating ability.

STEP #3
Cold & Flu "Busting" Hydrotherapy Bath: This will help to increase your fever as necessary, helping to facilitate what it is already trying to do, which is speed up your immune system and speed up your healing. (See page 60 for how to do it.)

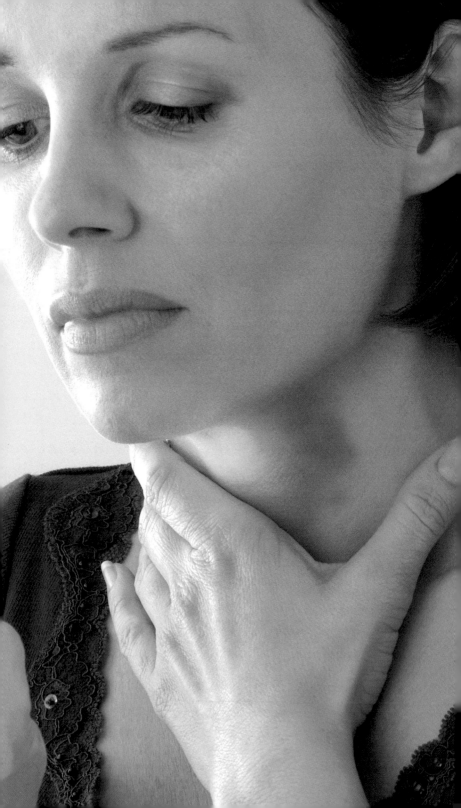

CHAPTER 8
TREATING SORE THROATS AND TONSILLITIS

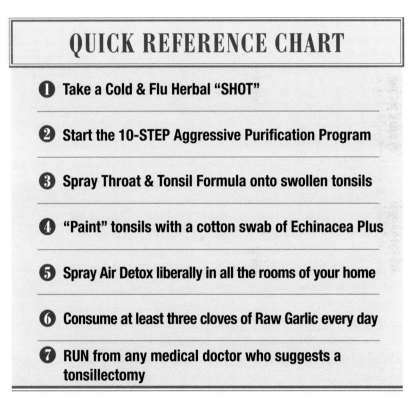

QUICK REFERENCE CHART

1. Take a Cold & Flu Herbal "SHOT"

2. Start the 10-STEP Aggressive Purification Program

3. Spray Throat & Tonsil Formula onto swollen tonsils

4. "Paint" tonsils with a cotton swab of Echinacea Plus

5. Spray Air Detox liberally in all the rooms of your home

6. Consume at least three cloves of Raw Garlic every day

7. RUN from any medical doctor who suggests a tonsillectomy

For some, a sore throat can be the worst part of a cold or flu infection, and the most painful. For many, it is their first sign that they have been infected and are coming down with a cold or flu. This is simply because the tonsils and adenoids are one of our first defenses against infections—and when they swell up, and become painful, that is simply because a battle line is being drawn there, and the battle is being waged, between your immune system, your immune cells, and the *invader*. Anything you can do now to assist your defense forces is really appreciated by your immune system. So, let's get in there and do some extra healing.

STEP #1

As you may remember, the first thing to do at the first sign of any infection, was to shake, drink, gargle and swallow one bottle of my **Cold & Flu Herbal "SHOT"**. This will not only stimulate and assist your immune system to do its job, but also to KILL any harmful bacterial and viral microbes that are lurking around in your throat.

STEP #2

Next, I would follow all the **10 Steps in my "Aggressive Purification" for Cold and Flu Program.** (See page 55.)

If your sore throat is bad, and you need some extra assistance, I HAVE LOTS OF IT!

STEP #3

First, I would spray some of my **Throat & Tonsil Spray** right on those swollen tonsils, at least a couple of good pumps on each tonsil. So, let's start by looking to see where your tonsils actually are…

It is best if you have a small, but bright flashlight (like some type of high intensity penlight), and of course, stand in front of the mirror while you are doing this. You can even use a standing or bathroom magnification mirror. Now open your mouth, stick your tongue all of the way out and even say the cliché "ahhhhh". This will stretch out and also depress the tongue down even further and this usually exposes the tonsils even more. If you need more exposure, a popsicle stick will do the trick, or any long thin and flat object that can be used as a tongue depressor. I have used many a toothbrush end during an emergency housecall, when I didn't have my bag with me. And you can even buy tongue depressors, which are the best at any pharmacy.

Anyway, when you do this you will usually see three things; your tongue, your tonsils on either side of the back of your tongue and your uvula (the single sack that hangs down from your soft palate or the roof of your mouth, in the middle of your throat).

If your tonsils are infected, swollen and painful, well, they will be easy to see and will look enlarged, have swollen red veins on them, probably have pus oozing out of them and will look as sore as they feel.

Now, simply spray a few pumps of the **Throat & Tonsil Spray** directly onto each tonsil. Try not to breathe in as you are doing this, as there is no need to inhale the **Throat & Tonsil Spray** into your lungs. And, try not to touch your uvula (described earlier) with the tongue depressor, as this will almost always cause gagging and if done enough, vomiting.

The **Throat & Tonsil Spray** may sting a bit on your tonsils at first, but this will immediately be taken over by its natural Peppermint and Echinacea, which will cool and numb the pain and give you the desired relief from the soreness. Better yet, the Echinacea and Cayenne will start boosting your immune system circulation immediately and the Garlic will kill the bacteria and virus on contact! Your tonsils will love you for doing this.

STEP #4
"Painting" Your Tonsils

For more direct and intensive treatment to the tonsils, you can treat them by using more herbal medicine DIRECTLY on the tonsils. In the old days, natural doctors used to call this routine application *painting* the tonsils. Now I am no artist, but I have "painted" many tonsils in my day, so here is how to do it. All you need is a mirror (if you are doing it to yourself), a small flashlight and some cotton swabs (the longer ones from the pharmacy are best as they are easier to reach the tonsils with). You can also tape two of them together, or tape one on to the end of a stick or pencil, so you can easily reach the tonsils. I have also used a natural bristle paint brush, which is how the name "painting" the tonsils came about. All of them are easy to do.

Next, saturate the cotton at the end of a cotton bud, swab or bristles of the brush with **Echinacea Plus**, until it is dripping with it. Holding the flashlight in one hand, put the **Echinacea Plus** saturated cotton swab into your mouth and way back onto your tonsil. It is best if you can even gently push it right into your tonsil openings and crevices. This may hurt for only a split second, but the **Echinacea Plus** will numb the pain very quickly. Repeat this and get the tonsils covered. If you are a real trooper, you can also soak a cotton swab with my **SuperTonic** and repeat this same routine, after the **Echinacea Plus**, which will immediately KILL any bacteria and virus, but will also burn a little.

Between gargling with your **Cold & Flu Herbal "SHOTS"**, and using your **Throat & Tonsil Spray**, and even "painting" your tonsils with my **Echinacea Plus** and also my **SuperTonic**, the germs and the infection won't stand a chance. Better yet, you can stop the infection right at ground zero, before it spreads any further.

OK, here is an even more intensive routine. During bad tonsil inflammation (when a patient was in a lot of pain and agony), I have even "painted on" my **Deep Tissue Oil** or **Ointment**, right onto the tonsils, and this has offered amazing relief.

In fact, it is well known that this is often the first location for the infection, and that as it drips down with gravity helping it, that this infection is then carried into the lungs. Ending the battle right here and now with some natural and aggressive tonsil treatment can save you a lot of pain and suffering, and keep you from getting a lung infection altogether.

STEP #5

Spray my **Air Detox** liberally all around you. It will kill the airborne bacteria and virus that is attacking you. Spray it on your pillow to protect you and help you breathe all night long.

STEP #6

Consume at least three cloves of Raw Garlic every day (yes, children, too)! Garlic is the most powerful broad-spectrum antibiotic and antiviral around. Some of my adult patients took over 50 cloves a day when they were very ill so don't wimp out with taking Garlic.

It is simply a miracle healer for tonsillitis!

STEP #7

RUN from any ignorant medical doctor or pediatrician that suggests a tonsillectomy.

FINALLY...

Remember, curing diseases naturally by assisting your body and immune system to do its job, EDUCATES your immune system. Your immune system has a memory and will know how to deal with this germ the next time around. Doctors, drugs and surgery do not EDUCATE your body or immune system. They damage your body and leave your immune system ignorant or impaired.

The only real cure to any disease is you taking RESPONSIBILITY for yourself and your health. Create a healthy lifestyle and your body can heal itself of anything. Just STOP doing what is making you sick and START doing what Creates Powerful Health, and dis-ease will leave your body in a hurry.

What Are Your Tonsils? Do They Have Any Purpose?

The following is everything you ever wanted to know about your tonsils *that your medical doctor will never, ever tell you.*

Look, every fall, winter and spring, hundreds of thousands of American children and adults get tonsillitis. Just recently, a number of customers in the pharmacy asked me about tonsillitis. One female customer had two kids at home with tonsillitis and another customer (a grown man) had it himself. Both were told by their medical doctors to have their tonsils removed. I was shocked that still in this day and age, greedy, ignorant medical doctors are still butchering people and cutting out tonsils, when all the medical immunology textbooks now teach that **the tonsils are extremely important parts of our immune system. In fact, medical immunology textbooks actually caution that tonsil removal will impair the body's immune system.** (I will quote them later.)

The bottom line is that I want you to be armed with some good information about these organs, the next time some ignorant family member, friend, school teacher or nurse, or medical doctor, suggests removing them.

What are the tonsils?

The word tonsil comes from the Latin *tonsilla*, which means "almond". According to Taber's Cyclopedic Medical Dictionary the tonsils are defined as, "a mass of **lymphoid tissue** in the mucous membranes of the pharynx (throat)." **Lymphoid tissue** consists of lymphocytes, which are white blood cells (the major part of your body's immune system). So in plain English, the **tonsils are almond shaped sacs of immune tissue in the throat that contain white blood cells**. They are connected to and part of your immune system.

Do you have more than one set of tonsils?

YES. You actually have three sets of tonsils, the lingual, the palatine and the pharyngeal (adenoids). The only one you can really see are the palatine. You have two, one on either side, where the back of the mouth meets the throat. The ones you can't see are the pharyngeal (adenoids), which are way up in the back of your throat near your sinus cavity, and the lingual which are on the far back of your tongue. *It was like God knew that some idiot medical doctors were going to cut them off, so a few extra pair were hidden out of sight, and out of reach!*

Do they have any purpose?

Anyone who asks that question is not a believer in God, nature or even evolution. Why would the human body have anything in it that we don't need or that doesn't have a purpose? Only ignorant people suggest that we have parts and organs in our bodies that *don't have any purpose or that we don't need.*

Often, you will hear ignorant medical doctors or scientists say that the tonsils serve no purpose. More accurately, what they mean to say is that they have no idea what they are, that they were sleeping at their desk during that year of advanced immunology in medical school, and haven't read an updated medical immunology text in over 20 years. Because for over 20 years, EVERY medical book on immunology defines the tonsils as a very important part of your body's immune system.

What do they do?

As I stated earlier, your tonsils are lymphoid tissue that is rich in immune white blood cells. The majority of these cells (80%-90%) are T-cells and B-cells.

T-cells are a type of white blood cell that kills germs, bacteria, virus, fungus or anything that can hurt you. B-cells have different types of chemicals (immunoglobulin) on their surface that they use to make antibodies to poison and kill bacteria, virus and harmful organisms. Together these T-cells and B-cells get rid of the bacteria, virus and "bad guys" that enter your mouth and throat and help keep you healthy.

Why are my tonsils in my throat?

The nose and mouth are where we take in water, food and air. If while we are taking in this life-giving food, water and air we also take in harmful substances that can make us sick (like germs, bacteria, virus, fungus, etc.), it's the job of the tonsils to detect these germs and put up a fight. The tonsils are the main immune system protectors we have at the biggest opening into the human body. And in this area, they are usually the first defense when we inhale infected saliva or mucous "droplets" loaded with bacteria and virus from someone coughing or sneezing.

*"In this location, the tonsils provide an ever-present source of lymphocytes (white blood cells) capable of reacting against microbes that constantly bombard the oral cavity… **the tonsils are the body's first line of defense against microbes**… These characteristics underscore the importance of the tonsils in the maintenance of immunity and provide evidence that argues against performing a tonsillectomy."*
From "General Immunology" by Edwin L. Cooper

Today, medical doctors in America are still cutting 500,000 children's tonsils out every year. I have sometimes referred to medical doctors as greedy, ignorant and even butchers. At least two of these three words are accurate when it comes to removing the tonsils, and probably the third is also.

And there is more …

According to immunology medical books the tonsils are more important than most people could imagine. In fact, there is an increased incidence of Hodgkin's Disease and other types of cancer in persons who have had their tonsils cut out. And, according to immunology textbooks, there is also an increased incidence of paralytic poliomyelitis (polio) after a tonsillectomy stating that **"removal of the tonsils in young children impairs their anti-polio**

immune mechanism." Worse yet, the tonsils are the only known part of your immune system that has the capability to manufacture the antibody to fight poliomyelitis (polio).

Why do the tonsils get red, swollen, hurt and drain pus?

When this happens, it simply means that your tonsils are doing their job. The swelling is due to the rush and consequent congestion of white blood cells to the area. They are rushing there to fight off the invaders. Swollen tonsils means that you have been infected, and the battle between your immune system and the invading germs, bacteria or virus is on. This is called tonsillitis or "tonsil inflammation".

Pictures From The Clinic

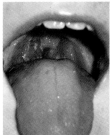

Swollen tonsils
accompanied by pus

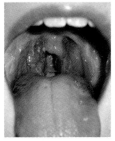

Tonsils so swollen they
are touching each other

I took these pictures of a child with severe tonsillitis, so you can clearly see the tonsils. Although I consider this severe tonsillitis, I had thousands of children in my clinic with tonsils that looked just like this. It is quite common. A person with tonsils this swollen will ache and be in pain, usually not feel well, and often will have a sore throat. The tonsils can look like this at the beginning, during or at the end of a cold. They can stay swollen for weeks, even after the patient feels better. Normally, you will not notice the tonsils when you look in someone's mouth. When they are this swollen, it is common to see pus, like in this picture. Pus is just dead "kamakazi" white blood cells after they kill bacteria or virus and eventually die themselves.

It is also common to see red engorged blood vessels, as in this picture. It is not uncommon to even have blood in the saliva or right on the tonsils.

To see the tonsils clearly, depress the tongue with a popsicle stick, use a flashlight to see in, and have the patient say "ahh", loudly, as they open their mouth up as wide as they can.

In the second picture, you can see that the tonsils are so swollen now, they are touching each other. This child was so uncomfortable they could hardly open their mouth. This is not as common of an occurrence, but I have seen this often too. It almost appears that the tonsils are blocking and closing off the airway. Do not fear, this will not happen. This patient had a hard time swallowing food, but not breathing. Someone with tonsillitis like this should not be eating food anyway, and on juices only.

The Link between Tonsillectomies, Polio, Cancer and even AIDS

There are a growing number of scientists and researchers that now believe that the entire polio epidemic was caused by foolish, ignorant and greedy medical doctors cutting out the tonsils of young children all across America.

In the 1920s, 30s and 40s medical doctors went on a huge campaign to remove children's tonsils. They even created family plans where you could bring all of your children into the doctor and have all of their tonsils removed, whether they were sick or not, and do it for a special money-saving price. By doing this, medical doctors cut out and removed the body's only immune defensive organ against polio in millions and millions of children. Soon after this massive tonsillectomy campaign, in the 1940s and 1950s, America was ravaged by a polio epidemic, now thought to have been directly caused by this medical tonsillectomy campaign folly.

It gets worse. By the 1950s, medical doctors and the press had frightened every parent and every child in America, and the fear was POLIO. Sounds like the Swine Flu "pandemic" scare, doesn't it? Then in 1955, the medical organizations, medical doctors and hospitals launched one of their largest and most financially lucrative campaigns ever, the supposed miracle polio vaccine. 300 million doses were forced on American children. It was made from infected, rotten animal pus, from monkey kidneys and other animals that were infected with poliomyelitis, and then killed. I am not even going to mention the other toxic ingredients here, but use your imagination, *it was the 1950s.*

This polio vaccine looked safe, using the best microscopes, tools and tests we had to examine it with, in the 1950s. But two decades later, in the 1970s, scientists again examined the polio vaccine, with more modern microscopes and tests that could look deeper and see more accurately, and the same Salk Polio Vaccine that medical doctors claimed was safe, that we gave to 300 million children in America (myself included) was IMMEDIATELY BANNED. It was found to be contaminated with approximately 150 other live viruses. Just one of these contaminants is the SV-40 virus.

In the beginning, in the 1950s, it was actually known that the Salk Vaccine was contaminated with the SV-40 virus. Both the Sabin vaccine (the "live virus" oral vaccine), and the Salk vaccine (the "killed virus" injectable vaccine) were known to be contaminated. But, extremely toxic and poisonous formaldehyde (embalming fluid) was added into the vaccine to deactivate and kill the SV-40 virus in the Salk vaccine. It was later discovered that this did NOT kill the SV-40 virus. Consequently, everyone that received the famous supposedly life-saving Salk Vaccine also received a dose of LIVE Monkey Kidney Pus SV-40 virus.

SV-40 is a Monkey Virus, also now found in humans. It is well documented to cause tumor growth in the human body. It is suspected that it has been one of the contributing factors in the dramatic increase in the cancer rate over the past 50 years and linked to many cancers from sarcomas to malignant mesothelioma.

Worse, recently at the Vaccine Cell Substrate Conference, it was released that even after we banned this vaccine it was still sold and used in the millions in former Soviet bloc countries and also in China, Japan and Africa, up to and possibly beyond 1980. Literally hundreds of millions of people are now known to have been exposed to this SV-40 Virus.

So, the SV-40 Monkey Virus was mistakenly injected into hundreds of millions. Also, the World Health Organization's forced Smallpox Eradication Inoculation Program, well, it was also found to be a contaminated "monkey" vaccine. Together, both of these vaccines have been used extensively in the Third World and both of these vaccines have also been linked to the cause of the spread of AIDS in Africa and many other Third World countries.

From tonsillectomies, to polio, to cancer, to AIDS, we will never know the truth behind this monstrous medical scandal, nor the impact and death toll brought on by this folly of medical doctors, pharmaceutical companies and government health organizations. And we will be dealing with the diseases and death for centuries. An old "Nature Cure" doctor once said to me, "It is a good idea to never break the seal of the body (the skin) with a needle and inject any man-made substances into it." A wise man!

CHAPTER 9
TREATING SINUS INFECTIONS AND BLOCKED SINUS

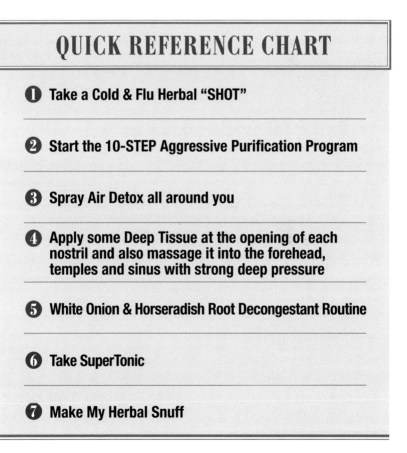

QUICK REFERENCE CHART

1 Take a Cold & Flu Herbal "SHOT"

2 Start the 10-STEP Aggressive Purification Program

3 Spray Air Detox all around you

4 Apply some Deep Tissue at the opening of each nostril and also massage it into the forehead, temples and sinus with strong deep pressure

5 White Onion & Horseradish Root Decongestant Routine

6 Take SuperTonic

7 Make My Herbal Snuff

STEP #1

Again, the first thing to do at the first sign of any infection, is to shake, drink, gargle and swallow one bottle of my **Cold & Flu Herbal "SHOT"**. This will not only stimulate and assist your immune system to do its job, but also to KILL any harmful bacterial and viral microbes that are lurking around in your throat. It also contains herbs like horseradish, to open up clogged sinuses.

STEP #2

Next, I would follow all the **10 Steps in my "Aggressive Purification" for Cold and Flu Program.** (See Chapter 6.)

STEP #3

Next, as I mentioned earlier, one great way to PREVENT cold and flu infections, is to spray my **Air Detox** everywhere around your home, car, office, wherever you are, to kill airborne cold and flu particles and droplets in the air and keep them from infecting you in the first place. But, if you have a stuffed up nose, head cold or even a lung infection, this formula is a real blessing. Use it liberally in your home, your shower or bath and even on your pillow at night.

STEP #4

You can also use my **Deep Tissue Ointment** as a chest rub at night for sinus infections, head colds, stuffed up and blocked nasal passages, as well as for lung congestion.

STEP #5

White Onion and Horseradish Root Sinus Decongestant Routine

I will never forget the female patient I had in my clinic 30 years ago. She was actually the wife of one of my male patients and I had never met her before. She didn't really believe in natural healing so she had avoided seeing me, even though her husband had healed his diseases using my methods.

Anyway, she had been out of work for a few weeks and was in desperate trouble. She had a chronic sinus infection and her sinus passages were completely blocked, 100%. She had gone to the medical doctor who, believe it or not, put hypodermic needles up her nose into her sinus cavity and injected drugs to kill the infection and unblock her nostrils and sinus—and all it seemed to do is break numerous blood vessels and give her two black eyes. She had not slept in three days and was physically, emotionally and spiritually broken, desperate, crying and couldn't breathe, had two black eyes and she broke down and begged for my help. So, her husband (my patient) brought her into my clinic.

I took her right into my office and laid her down on my examination table and told her to relax. I then took a very hot washcloth, soaked with hot water and placed it over her eyes, sinus and nostrils. I then took some **Air Detox** and sprayed it onto the washcloth (being careful not to get it into her eyes) and put a small dab of my **Deep Tissue Ointment** at the opening of each nostril and did some massage on her forehead and sinus, and quite strong deep pressure. After a few minutes, when she was much more relaxed and no longer hysterical, I asked her to come into my kitchen.

In my kitchen, I asked her to grate some fresh horseradish root and to chew and eat some of it while she was grating a whole root. Next, I asked her to chop some white onions for me, and also to eat a few of these white onions she was chopping. She was beginning to sweat a bit and tears were streaming down her cheeks. I then gave her a couple droppersful of my **SuperTonic**, which is basically more White Onion, more Horseradish root, with some Garlic juice and Cayenne peppers and Ginger root. I then asked her to take a deep breath for me through her sinuses, and sobbing, she said to me, "I can't." I persisted and when she tried, we could hear a little squeaking noise as her sinuses were in fact opening up. I said. "Let's go back into my office", where we repeated the hot wet washcloth, with the **Air Detox**, deep tissue massage, **Deep Tissue Ointment**, and then back out to the kitchen to grate and eat more Horseradish root, chop and eat more White Onions and consume more **SuperTonic**.

The long and short of this is that within about 15 minutes, her sinuses were completely unblocked and open. I told her to rest on my table, while I went out into the waiting room and told her husband he could go in and see her.

As I was cleaning up in the kitchen, I heard a big smash and then crash in my office, and I ran into find her crying, sobbing, she had thrown one of my textbooks, and was screaming something like, "I lost two weeks at work, I haven't sleep in three days, I have taken a hundred pills, and even had medical doctors stick needles up my nose and sinus, which hurt like hell and gave me two black eyes... and this guy cleared my sinuses in 10 minutes with Horseradish and Onions!!!" She was furious, not at me, but at the medical doctors and her own ignorance.

Anyway, Horseradish root and White Onions are powerful treatments to open up blocked sinus passages, even blocked tear ducts with Conjunctivitis. Beyond that, the odor of Onions, *and of course,* Garlic will kill the bacteria, virus and infection, too.

For years in my clinic, I would simply ask my patients with blocked nasal passages to start grating up some fresh Horseradish root and chop up some fresh White Onions and also to chew and eat some of the grated and chopped foods, and this would open up the most blocked up nasal passages.

STEP #6
SuperTonic

Every herbalist seems to make their own "plague" or "worst-case scenario" tonic, and mine is my **SuperTonic**. It contains Garlic and Onions that will kill any bacteria, virus, fungus or anything that is harmful to you. It also contains Horseradish root to drive all of this healing power and phytochemicals up to your head, and of course Habanero peppers and Ginger rhizome to blast your circulation and get all of these healing plant chemicals throughout your head, throat and chest.

My patients simply called it: "The Cure for the Common Cold." It is simply a concentrated tonic of the "Onion and Horseradish Routine" in the previous section, plus more herbs!

STEP #7
My Herbal Snuff

I wanted to give you one additional secret weapon that I used to make in my clinic and use for the worst infected and blocked sinus problems. I used to make what I called my Herbal Snuff for my patients with blocked sinus passages and sinus infections, and I will give you the recipe right here…

Recipe:

Take about a teaspoon of Goldenseal root powder and a teaspoon of Bayberry bark powder, and make sure they are finely sifted powders and put them into a small jar. Next, add a "pinch'" of Garlic powder or granules, I find the granules stronger, and also a "pinch" of Cayenne powder. Now, no bitching or whining here by you people who want exact recipes, because this is my *exact* recipe. In fact, I am a pinch and a handful kind of guy and my company has spent years trying to decode my clinical formulas and turn them into scientific measurements. Anyway, I say a "pinch" and you will understand when you use it, a little pinch for the beginners and a big pinch for the Natural Healing adventurers. Then, shake up all these ingredients in a jar and mix them well.

1 teaspoon	Goldenseal root powder (fine powder)
1 teaspoon	Bayberry bark powder (fine powder)
1 pinch	Cayenne pepper
1 pinch	Garlic granules (more potent than powder)

Put the contents into a small jar, shake it and mix well before use.

Dosage

For infected sinuses, take a pinch of this powder and snuff it deeply up into your sinus passages, and do it powerfully as you only have the nerve to do it once. Then, hold on to something, because it will burn a bit—but, it will clear your sinuses and disinfect them good. Have fun!

I have used this a thousand times in my clinic for the most stubborn sinus infections and congestion, and it never failed my patients.

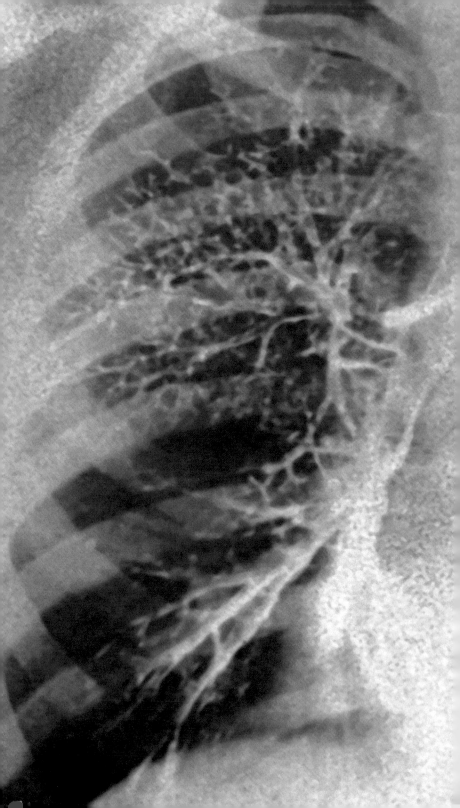

CHAPTER 10
TREATING LUNG INFECTIONS AND CONGESTION

QUICK REFERENCE CHART

1 Take a Cold & Flu Herbal "SHOT"

2 Start the 10-STEP Aggressive Purification Program

3 Spray Air Detox all around you

4 Take Lung Tonic

5 Apply Deep Tissue rubbed into the chest

STEP #1
My first and initial treatment for any cold or flu infection, even a cough and even when the infection is deep into the lungs, is my **Cold & Flu Herbal "SHOT"**. This is simply because I want to supercharge your immune system and destroy bacteria and viruses, immediately.

STEP #2
Next, I would follow all the **10 Steps in my "Aggressive Purification" for Cold and Flu Program.**

Lung infections should be taken very seriously for many reasons. One is that you can go months without food (I know I have when I was healing myself) and you can even go days without liquids, but you can only survive a few minutes without air. I hear people all the time taking about which nutrient is the most important. Vitamin A? Vitamin C? Well, it's neither of them. It is AIR! Air is by far the most primary nutrient to the human body and without it you are dead in minutes. So, any infection or illness or dis-ease that is inflaming, swelling up and clogging my lungs—well, I consider it as important as if it were clogging up my heart. So get AGGRESSIVE and get to work.

Additional Helpful Programs for Lung Congestion and Infection…

STEP #3
Air Detox

My **Air Detox** not only purifies the air, kills pathogens, germs, bacteria and virus, but it also is very helpful when it is inhaled from just spraying it in the room. Don't inhale it directly, just breathe it in the room, and it will kill infectious agents, while helping you to breathe easier.

STEP #4
Lung Tonic

This is a specific herbal formula for clearing, drying up and disinfecting the sinus passages and the lungs. It will also dilate your bronchial tubes to help you breathe much easier.

My **Lung Tonic** works in two main ways. First, the plant chemicals in this tonic will dilate your bronchial tubes, forcing them to open wider so you can breathe easier. Second, while most doctors prescribe drugs to stop you from coughing, I have added herbs to this tonic that actually promote coughing. That's because you need to get the mucous out of your lungs or you can literally drown. Plus, if you suppress your cough, it'll just make the whole experience last longer. In a nutshell, my **Lung Tonic** makes it easier to breathe, as well as to cough up and expectorate mucous.

STEP #5
Deep Tissue Ointment or Oil
This formula can take the PAIN of an infection away and let you sleep!

I could tell you a hundred uses for just colds and flu, that is one of the reasons my patients named this formula a "miracle in a bottle." For lung infections and congestion, rub it on your chest, right over your lungs, and even on your neck. The vapors will decongest your sinus and lungs. Dilute it with a little olive oil, if doing this on children. This is a GREAT bedtime routine and offers awesome relief all night long.

You can also rub it on your neck to relieve the pain of swollen tonsils and glands, which will increase the lymphatic circulation. Or, rub it on your back for sore muscles and "bone ache" when you have a fever, because during fevers often your bones and lower back can ache. **Deep Tissue Oil** will take the pain away and increase the circulation.

For sore throats, you can take a few droppersful in your mouth and let them drip down your throat. You can even carefully "paint" the ointment or the oil right on a swollen infected tonsil (see Chapter 8 on Tonsillitis).

If you have sinus pain and pressure, rub it anywhere on the head, temples, bridge of the nose, even up inside the mouth on the soft palate. Are you getting the idea yet? You are only limited by your imagination. This formula is especially great when you are sick and wake up in pain and can't get back to sleep. Rub it on the painful areas, and in a few minutes you will be back in dreamland.

FOOD

TOOLS

HERBAL
MEDICINE

Dr. Schulze's
ORIGINAL CLINICAL FORMULAE
Since 1979

SuperFood
P L U S

VITAMIN & MINERAL HERBAL CONCENTRATE

HERBAL SUPPLEMENT
NET WEIGHT: 14 OUNCES / 396 GRAMS

Over 100% Vitamins A, B, C & E! Over 500% Vitamin B12!

Dr. Schulze's
HERBAL CLINICAL FORMULAE

Cold&Flu
herbal
"SHOT"

Herbal Formulae That Work!

HERBAL SUPPLEMENT

Dr. Schulze's
ORIGINAL CLINICAL FORMULAE
Since 1979

ECH+
ECHINACEA PLUS

Herbal Formulae That Work!

HERBAL SUPPLEMENT
2 FL. OZ. / 60 ml

Dr. Schulz
HERBAL CLINICAL FORMULAE

THROAT
&
TONSIL

Herbal Formulae That

HERBAL SUPPLEMENT
2 FL. OZ. / 60 ml

CHAPTER 11
SUPPLY LIST FOR THE PREVENTION AND TREATMENT OF A COLD OR FLU

FOOD & HERBS:
For Colds & Flu

- ▶ 6 Bulbs of Organic, Raw Garlic

- ▶ 6 Organic Lemons

- ▶ 6 Organic Limes

- ▶ 2 to 20 Organic Cayenne Peppers

- ▶ 1 Organic Ginger Root

- ▶ 1 Organic Horseradish Root

- ▶ 2 Organic White Onions

- ▶ Organic Fresh Fruit and Vegetable Juice

- ▶ Herbal Tea

- ▶ 2 Gallons of Pure Distilled Water

For Potassium Broth

▶ 12 Organic Potatoes

▶ 6 Organic Whole Beets (with Dark Green stems)

▶ 12 Organic Carrots

▶ 6 Organic White Onions

▶ 10 Bulbs of Organic, Raw Garlic

▶ 4 Bunches of Organic Dark Greens (Beet Greens, Kale, Collard, Spinach, etc.)

For Herbal Snuff

▶ 1 Teaspoon Organic Goldenseal root (fine powder)

▶ 1 Teaspoon Organic Bayberry bark (fine powder)

▶ 1 Pinch Garlic Granules

▶ 1 Pinch Cayenne Powder

TOOLS:

▶ Dr. Schulze Sports Bottle

▶ Air Purifier (with HEPA Filter)

▶ Surgical Mask

▶ Juicer

▶ Blankets

▶ Enema Bag

▶ High-Intensity Penlight Flashlight

▶ Tongue Depressors (or popsicle sticks)

- Bathroom Magnification Counter Mirror

- Long Cotton Swabs

- Natural Bristle Paint Brush (small)

HERBAL MEDICINE:
For Colds & Flu

- 1 SuperFood Plus

- 2 Cold & Flu Herbal "SHOT" (6-packs)

- 2 Echinacea Plus

- 1 SuperTonic

- 1 Throat & Tonsil Spray

- 1 Lung Tonic

- 2 Air Detox (2-oz.)

- 1 Cayenne Tincture

- 1 Deep Tissue Ointment or Oil

For Constipation

- 1 Intestinal Formula #1

- 1 Bowel Flush "SHOT" (3-pack)

For Cleansing & Detoxification

- 5-Day BOWEL Detox

- 5-Day LIVER Detox

- 5-Day KIDNEY Detox

CHAPTER 12
8 ESSENTIAL HERBAL MEDICINES FOR THE COLD & FLU SEASON

SuperFood Plus

BOTANICAL INGREDIENTS:

Spirulina Algae, Blue-Green Algae, Chlorella Broken-Cell Algae, Barley, Alfalfa and Wheat Grasses, Purple Dulse Seaweed, Acerola Cherry, Beet Root, Spinach Leaf, Rose Hips, Orange and Lemon Peels, Palm Fruit, in a base of Dr. Schulze's Proprietary *Non-Fermentable* Saccharomyces cerevisiae nutritional yeast

MEDICINAL ACTION:

Because it is made only from live food and herbs, Dr. Schulze's SuperFood Plus is highly *recognizable* by your body, which makes it highly *assimilable* by your digestive tract. In fact, some of the single-celled nutrients like the spirulina, chlorella and blue-green algae don't even have to be digested—they can be assimilated right into your body from your mouth. Consequently, this highly-concentrated nutritional complex literally *blasts* your bloodstream with a rich supply of vitamins and nutrients that create powerful energy, vitality and strength.

Most people today live on a diet of overprocessed and overcooked junk food, not to mention coffee, sugar, chocolate, alcohol, tobacco and prescription drugs, plus add in unheard of levels of stress, a lack of sleep and exercise and a toxic environment. **Modern life in general causes your immune system to fight a constant uphill battle, and this constant battle wears your immune system down. And, even if you live a healthy life, you need a constant high-level supply of readily available vitamins, especially during** cold and flu season. These nutrients are the building blocks of immune cells, immune chemicals and assure you that your immune system runs at peak performance.

Every patient who walked into Dr. Schulze's clinic was nutritionally depleted. A lack of nutrition in your blood can cause everything from low energy and a weak immune system to virtually any disease. Nutrition is what builds every cell, every organ and every metabolic chemical in your body—it's what YOU are made of. **Having a rich supply of nutrition in your blood gives you energy, vitality and strength; protects you from disease and illness and if you get sick, speeds up your recovery dramatically.**

SUGGESTED DOSAGE:

SuperFood Plus Powder

Dr. Schulze suggests two rounded tablespoons of **SuperFood Plus** in a morning "blender" drink, made with either fresh fruit or vegetable juice. If you have a cold or flu infection, he suggests a second dose in the afternoon.

SuperFood Plus Tablets

Dr. Schulze suggests taking 15 tablets in the morning with your breakfast nutritional drink. You can also spread them throughout the day, taking 5 tablets in the morning, 5 in the afternoon and the last 5 in the late afternoon. Remember, if you have a cold or flu infection, he suggests to double up and take 30 tablets throughout the day.

SuperFood Bar

Have it anytime throughout the day, and again, if you are infected, have an additional bar in the late afternoon for that double dose.

Dr. Schulze suggests using a double, even a triple dose if you have a cold or flu infection, or if you are anemic, have a low blood count or any illness or disease.

Cold & Flu Herbal "SHOT"

BOTANICAL INGREDIENTS:

Echinacea angustifolia root, Echinacea purpurea seed, Fresh Garlic bulb and juice, Habanero, Onions, Ginger, Horseradish, Acerola Cherry, Elderberry, Blackberry, Yarrow, Boneset, Desert Sage, Lobelia, Elecampane, Kola Nut, Licorice, Cherry Bark, Horehound, Coltsfoot, Fennel, Coffee and Thyme

MEDICINAL ACTION:

For years in his clinic, to prevent and treat cold and influenza infections, Dr. Schulze had his patients make a powerful healing drink with his Echinacea Plus tonic and his powerful SuperTonic. **Now, Dr. Schulze has pre-blended these two most powerful formulae to strengthen your body's natural immune defenses against seasonal attacks and fight bacteria, viruses and the germs that cause colds and influenza.**

He also added many other potent herbs for colds and flu and a maximum dose of Acerola Cherry juice to give you 1,000% (10 times) your needed Vitamin C, which is a powerful cold and flu infection fighter and blended this all into one formula: Dr. Schulze's **Cold & Flu Herbal "SHOT"**!

For specific medicinal action, see the action under **Echinacea Plus**, **SuperTonic** and **Lung Tonic**, because this tonic has all of these actions, plus it has diaphoretic herbs to make you sweat and assist you when you have a fever, and many herbs for your sinus and lungs, too.

SUGGESTED DOSAGE:

The dosage is one bottle. Simply shake the bottle, open it, gargle about half of the contents and swallow. Repeat this using the remaining contents of the "SHOT".

For serious cold and influenza infections, you can use two, three or up to six bottles a day.

Echinacea Plus

BOTANICAL INGREDIENTS:

Echinacea Angustifolia Root, Echinacea Purpurea Seed, Fresh Garlic Bulb, Fresh Habanero Pepper and Juice

MEDICINAL ACTION:

Echinacea Plus (ECH+) is a very powerful herbal tonic that wakes up your immune system. It stimulates and enhances the overall system, and can literally increase the number of immune cells and immune chemicals in the body. It's the best herbal offense to prevent colds and flu, and the best herbal defense, if you have been infected.

Echinacea has been scientifically proven to measurably increase the number of immune cells in your body, like macrophages, killer T-cells, B-cells, granulocytes and important immune chemicals that combat infection and disease.

Echinacea Plus (ECH+) stimulates these immune cells into heightened activity levels. Echinacea also significantly increases phagocytosis—your white blood cells' ability to destroy harmful micro-organisms such as bacteria, viruses and fungi. These actions will help you combat infection and disease more effectively while also protecting you from future invasions and illness.

Echinacea's effectiveness is clearly documented in respected medical textbooks such as The Merck Index and the Physician's Desk Reference for greatly reducing the severity of cold and flu infections, and also greatly reducing the length of them. That means that you will feel a lot better and get well a lot quicker using this remarkable immune system herbal blend.

SUGGESTED DOSAGE:

Like all of Dr Schulze's liquid herbal formulas, the standard dosage is two droppersful, three times per day.

That said, if you are infected, he suggests 6 to 12 droppersful up to six times a day, which means that you can consume an entire 2-ounce bottle per day in serious infections. You can use this formula liberally and as needed. There is no limit to the dosage.

SuperTonic

BOTANICAL INGREDIENTS:
Fresh, Raw Organic Horseradish Root, Organic Garlic Bulb, Organic White Onion, Organic Hawaiian Yellow Ginger Root and Organic Habanero Pepper

MEDICINAL ACTION:
This is Dr. Schulze's all-purpose herbal tonic with an almost unlimited list of uses.

His patients called it "The Cure for the Common Cold," but also often said it was the cure for EVERYTHING, and they used it in a thousand different ways.

SuperTonic destroys harmful micro-organisms that cause cold and flu infections, like bacteria and virus, ON CONTACT. It naturally breaks up sinus and chest congestion and infection, to promote open and clear breathing.

The FRESH JUICES of organic Horseradish root drive this formula to your head, sinus, throat and lungs, where you need it. The organic Garlic juice and its next of kin, organic Onion juice, are the two best herbs to destroy and flush harmful micro-organisms from your body *(see the "Four Thieves Vinegar" under Garlic's History in this book)*. The organic Yellow Ginger root juice and organic Habanero pepper juice stimulate your blood and lymphatic flow like no other herbs. This gets your immune cells to the infection as fast as possible. The organic, raw, unfiltered Apple Cider Vinegar preserves all of these plant juices and cleanses your body, too.

SUGGESTED DOSAGE:
Put about 8 droppersful in a shot glass. Use undiluted, gargle then swallow. You can use this formula liberally and as needed, there is no limit to the dosage.

Throat & Tonsil Spray

BOTANICAL INGREDIENTS:
Echinacea Angustifolia Root, Echinacea Purpurea Seed, Garlic Bulb, Habanero Pepper, Peppermint Leaf and Essential Oil, Peppermint Spirits, California Fig Concentrate

MEDICINAL ACTION:
Doctors agree that the flu and most colds start in your sinuses and throat. Then, the dripping infection drains downward and infects your lungs, and then you really get sick. If you can stop the infection early—while it is still in your throat—you will save yourself a lot of pain and suffering.

Dr. Schulze's **Throat & Tonsil Spray,** with its powerful Echinacea blend and Peppermint Spirits makes it powerfully cooling and numbing for great relief to sore throats and tonsillitis. Most important, it destroys the bacterial and viral infection on contact. This is the best way for you to defend against the micro-organisms that cause cold and influenza infections, tonsillitis and sore throats.

SUGGESTED DOSAGE: Spray 8 times directly into the back of your throat to saturate your throat and tonsils. Repeat as often as necessary. Shake well before each use.

Lung Tonic

BOTANICAL INGREDIENTS:
Lobelia Leaf and Seed, Elecampane Root, Coltsfoot Leaf, Horehound Leaf, Licorice Root, Kola Nut, Coffee Bean, Cherry Bark, Thyme Leaf, Fennel Seed, Peppermint Leaf Essential Oil

MEDICINAL ACTION:

Dr. Schulze's Lung Tonic has two principle functions. First, it helps dilate your bronchial tubes, which are the airways to your lungs. This will naturally help you to breathe easier. This will also help you to expectorate mucous from your lungs. Secondly, Dr. Schulze's Lung Tonic also reduces inflammation in your lungs and promotes healing.

During any lung infection, there are two things that you can do that will help you get better much more rapidly. First, stop consuming ALL dairy products. They are well known for congesting the lungs and sinus. Consume only pure water, fresh juices and herbal teas until you are well. Second, use Dr. Schulze's **Cold & Flu Herbal "SHOT"** along with the **Lung Tonic** to supercharge your immune system.

SUGGESTED DOSAGE:

60 drops (2 droppersful) to 120 drops (4 droppersful) in two ounces of water or juice, two to eight times daily.

Air Detox

BOTANICAL INGREDIENTS:

100% pure essential oils of Eucalyptus, Grapefruit, Lime, Lemon and Orange

MEDICINAL ACTION:

Dr. Schulze originally developed this formula specifically to disinfect the air in his clinic. With many terminally ill and very sick patients—some literally crawling or being carried through the door—his clinic sometimes smelled horrible and the air was thick with germs. Only pure, undiluted 100% essential oils are strong enough to disinfect the air and kill bacteria, viruses and fungi, especially in the bathroom. **These pure botanical essential oils are not some flowery cover-up, they are full-spectrum antimicrobial and effective broad-spectrum bactericide, fungicide, antiviral and antiparasitic.** His interns would spray this formula about every 10 minutes in his waiting room and examination rooms.

In your home, this "industrial-strength" formula will ensure that the air you are breathing is both disease-free and infection-free. **It kills the bacteria that cause the common cold and the virus that causes the flu. It is essential for high-risk households with children, pregnant women and senior citizens.** It is a full-strength blend of very powerful essential oils that destroy airborne pathogens and harmful micro-organisms on contact.

Dr. Schulze designed this blend not only to be the most powerful germ-killing formula, **but also for the aromatherapy action of lifting the spirits of the ill and refreshing our minds.** Our ancestors used these herbs for their medicinal value, as well as for their emotional and spiritual value. These herbs were also used to cleanse the living environment of bad feelings and negative energy.

FOR EXTERNAL USE ONLY:
Spray 1 to 6 times high into the air to disinfect and purify the area.

Deep Tissue Ointment or Oil

BOTANICAL INGREDIENTS:
Wintergreen Oil, Botanical Menthol, Habanero Pepper, Arnica Flower, Calendula Flower, St. John's Wort Flower, Extra Virgin Olive Oil, Natural Unbleached Beeswax

MEDICINAL ACTION:
For years in his clinic, Dr. Schulze made many powerfully effective topical ointments and oils. Two of his most famous were his maximum strength Deep *Heating* Oil, which was his Masters Thesis in Herbal College, and his Deep *Tissue Repair* Oil, both of which were used by top athletic competitors around the world. *One day, he decided to mix these two formulae together, and that's when the healing miracles really started to happen.*

The herbal ingredients in his Deep *Heating* Oil were pure Wintergreen Oil, Botanical Menthol and Habanero Pepper. These herbs are famous for **reducing inflammation, decreasing pain and increasing circulation, which all promote faster healing.**

The herbal ingredients in his Deep *Tissue Repair* Oil were Arnica Flower, Calendula Flower and St. John's Wort Flower; **all world-famous for healing bruises, bangs, trauma, torn muscles, tendons, ligaments and even fractured and broken bones.** Together these two oil formulae became much greater than the individual oils.

Dr. Schulze's **Deep Tissue Ointment and Oil** is amazing for arthritis, bursitis, painful bone and joint diseases, stiffness, injuries of all kinds, broken and fractured bones, sprains, strains, bruises and almost any healing of the body. Rub it on the temples for headaches or for cold and flu, and put it on the head or chest for congestion. That two-week recovery will only be a few days. The next morning, you will see the amazing healing that has taken place.

SUGGESTED DOSAGE:
For topical use only. Apply as needed. Rub in well for 10 minutes. Do not use near eyes, mucous membranes or genital area.

CHAPTER 13
GENERAL INFORMATION

GARLIC:
Garlic's History

With my own personal life-saving healing as a kid, and also with my patients in the clinic, I have learned well that Garlic is truly a miracle plant. If I were to be restricted to only a handful of herbs, Garlic, Cayenne, Lobelia and Aloe would be on the top of the list, and in that order!

For powerful health, start adding raw Garlic into your food program. Take it easy at first and finely chop up little pieces and sneak them into your food. In no time, you will probably become a Garlic junkie like myself and start eating large amounts of it. When I cook (actually heat food and cook), I will add four to six BULBS or about 100 cloves of Garlic to a curry or a pasta sauce that I am making for three or four people. When cooking with Garlic, don't be a wimp. Heat destroys a lot of Garlic's odor, taste, intensity and *medicinal action*, so always use a lot more of it if you are going to cook it. When visiting Los Angeles or San Francisco, try eating at the Stinking Rose Restaurant to experience some of the possibilities of Garlic cuisine.

Since it is my favorite healing herb and also one of my favorite foods, I would like to tell you a little more about Garlic's medicinal power. This may encourage you to add more of this wonderful, miraculous and healing plant into your life. By the way, a great healing dose is at least three cloves of FRESH, RAW Garlic every day.

Garlic and Disease-causing Micro-Organisms

Garlic is a very powerful antibiotic, antiviral and antifungal agent. Garlic juice diluted one part in 125,000 has been found to inhibit the growth of bacteria. In fact, even just the odor of garlic has been proven in the laboratory to be a powerful disease and infection-destroying agent, effectively killing germs.

An Effective and Safe Broad-Spectrum Antibiotic

Garlic destroys BOTH gram-positive and gram-negative bacteria, making it a natural **broad-spectrum antibiotic.** Garlic's successful long-term use as an antibacterial agent in Russia has awarded it the nickname of Russian Penicillin.

Pharmaceutical antibiotics are nonselective in their destruction of bacteria in your body—they just destroy it all. This creates many problems, because our body has many so-called *friendly* bacteria that we need for proper metabolic functions. This is why many people, after a course of antibiotic therapy, have digestive problems, constipation and yeast and fungal infections. Our bodies also become immune to these antibiotics over time and sometimes, dangerous resistant strains of bacteria are actually created in our body. Today there are many of these "flesh-eating" and other unstoppable bacteria that have been linked to the indiscriminate use of antibiotics.

Garlic is totally selective in its bacteria destruction, killing only the harmful bacteria in your body. What is amazing is that at the same time, garlic actually enhances your friendly bacteria and improves your intestinal flora and digestion.

Garlic destroys many types of bacteria, including *streptococcus, staphylococcus, typhoid, diphtheria, cholera, bacterial dysentery (traveler's diarrhea), tuberculosis, tetanus, rheumatic bacteria* and many others.

An Effective Anti-Viral Medicine

Garlic destroys, on contact, the viral infections of *influenza, rhino-virus, measles, mumps, mononucleosis, chicken pox, herpes simplex #1 and #2, herpes zoster, viral hepatitis, scarlet fever, rabies* and others.

Some say that the reason you don't catch colds when you eat Garlic is because no one will come near you. But in fact, Garlic is also a powerful anti-viral agent. Many feel it's the cure for the common cold, because it destroys the numerous viruses that cause upper-respiratory infections and influenza.

Garlic is a powerful anti fungal medicine also, both internally and externally. It has been shown in history, in the field, in the laboratory and in the clinic to be a potent and powerful healing medicine. It is a great health-building food, because it increases power and energy in the body, along with being a powerful healer and a powerful medicine for colds and influenza.

Covering Up the Odor

My father was a bus driver and I occasionally remember him coming home at night, complaining about someone who got on his bus, and then he had to smell *second-hand* garlic all across town. It is a funny thing, but if you haven't had garlic, the odor of someone who has had it can be offensive. In my clinic, I made all of my patients use a lot of garlic. Whether it was their Liver/Gallbladder Flush Drink or as part of my cancer routines, most of my patients reeked of garlic at one time or another.

So, when you use garlic, whether for culinary fun or medicine, you will get garlic breath. Another thing I have never seen work in my clinic was digestive pills or supplements like parsley oil pills or chlorophyll that *supposedly* when ingested will eliminate garlic's odor on your breath. As my Italian friends say, "forget about it". It does NOT work. The only thing that I find that works is to cover up the smell of garlic on your breath with strong essential plant oils, like peppermint. So that is why I designed my **Fresh Breath Plus** herbal breath tonic. Mainly to cover up and hide the odor of garlic on the breath of my patients, so they could do their healing and health-building, and still have friends and a social life. Many of them were in the entertainment industry or business leaders, so they simply couldn't walk around all day with "dragon breath". Their breath had to smell great no matter how much garlic they consumed, and my **Fresh Breath Plus** herbal breath tonic completely covered up garlic's odor.

What About Odorless Garlic?

Now before you even go there, the odor in garlic is bound to the most medicinal phytochemicals in garlic, especially allicin. So don't even think about odorless or odor free garlic supplements. No matter what they claim, I have NEVER, EVER seen any of them be effective for healing and treating disease in my clinic, PERIOD!

Also, there is a good reason I told my patients to chop it and chew it. See garlic doesn't actually contain any allicin at all, unless you chop it or chew it. Allicin (just one of the amazing medicinal chemicals in garlic) is actually formed by breaking garlic down or cutting it. Garlic has liquid cells and fibrous cells and when you cut or chew it, the enzyme allinase reacts to the alliin, both natural chemicals in garlic, and converts the alliin into allicin. And again, allicin is the major antibacterial, anti-viral, anti-fungal and anti *everything* property of garlic and is also the *odor* of garlic.

A History of the Medicinal Use of Garlic

Garlic, known botanically as *Allium sativum*, is certainly one of nature's miracle plants. It has been worshipped since the beginning of recorded history for its ability to heal and strengthen the body. The ancient Egyptians, Greeks and Romans all used garlic in copious amounts to increase strength and combat disease and illness. It was a favorite of Spartan warriors, and the Roman Centurions and Infantry. Even prior to this, the Egyptians gave it to the laborers who built the pyramids. It has been used for strength, stamina and power throughout history.

Hippocrates, the so-called father of modern medicine, was actually an herbalist and natural healer. He used garlic specifically to treat cancer.

Garlic was also known to both prevent and even cure the plagues of Europe. It was the main ingredient in the famous "Four Thieves Vinegar", which was a vinegar consumed by robbers during the French plagues who never got ill, even after robbing the dead bodies of plague victims.

As recently as World War I and II, when there was a shortage of sulfur drugs to treat battle wounds, the British government came to the rescue using garlic in the battlefield hospitals. British field doctors used fresh chopped Garlic and/or Garlic juice and spread it on sphagnum moss and applied it directly onto battlefield wounds. It is reported in British Medical Journals that whenever this treatment was applied, it always stopped the infection and is credited with saving thousands of lives. During both World Wars it was used in various other preparations to disinfect and heal battle wounds, and also used internally to successfully treat typhoid fever and dysentery.

Today, garlic is the leading over-the-counter drug in many European and Asian countries. It is an official drug in many countries and prescribed by medical doctors outside the U.S. for many diseases, including hypertension (high blood pressure), high cholesterol, cancer and especially as a broad-spectrum antibiotic, antiviral agent and fungicide.

It was eliminated from medical use during the last century in the United States, not because of its inability to heal, but due to pressure on doctors from the American Medical Association and the pharmaceutical companies. For years, the pharmaceutical industry and the AMA have been attempting to discourage the public from using plants to heal themselves, in fact discouraging any self-treating of disease, to make you more dependent on medical doctors and drugs. It seems that even the tight fist from these two groups and two trillion dollars they demand every year, can't keep Garlic underground anymore.

What's Wrong With The Flu Shot? EVERYTHING!

#1: The ingredients in the flu shot are toxic and disgusting!

First, the basis of the flu shot is animal pus. They take animals and infect them with last year's flu strain, and then kill them. When the animals die and rot, they take the pus (which has the antibodies) and mix that with extremely poisonous antifreeze and a few other things like formaldehyde (which is embalming fluid), highly-toxic carbolic acid (which is one of the biggest poisons known), aluminum (which causes seizures and, of course, is directly linked to be the cause of dementia and Alzheimer's disease), and then they add some mercury in as a preservative (which we know is a toxic heavy metal that causes nerve damage, liver damage and cancer).

Poisons found in the typical flu vaccine…

- Ethylene Glycol: Used as automobile antifreeze

- Carbolic Acid: A toxic, caustic poison

- Formaldehyde: Embalming fluid that causes cancer

- Aluminum: Causes Alzheimer's disease, seizures and cancer

- Mercury: Extremely toxic heavy metal that kills brain, nerve and immune cells and whose use in the vaccine preservative, Thimerosal, is linked to many childhood brain and nerve diseases, including autism

#2: Influenza viruses are constantly mutating!

According to the Center for Disease Control, "Influenza seasons are unpredictable. The beginning, severity, and length of an epidemic can vary widely from year to year making it impossible to accurately predict the features of any season."

Even the pharmaceutical manufacturers admit, "This is a serious problem and places serious doubts on the effectiveness of any influenza vaccine."

Even worse, as you have read in this book already, influenza viruses are in constant fluctuation, constantly "drifting" and "shifting" and mutating into new and different varieties and strains, which makes it literally impossible to make a specific poison for. This is why in Natural Healing, we simply get you extremely healthy and strong, and super-charge your own immune system, and then let it figure out exactly what the viral or bacterial invader is and make its own natural "poison" to kill it. This is safer, more effective and accurate, and maybe best, lets your immune system "educate" itself.

#3: Facts prove the flu shot doesn't work!
A few decades ago, less than 20,000 people a year died from the flu. Last year, it was over 40,000!

Dr. J. Anthony Morris (former Chief Vaccine Control Officer at the FDA) states: *"There is no evidence that any influenza vaccine thus far developed is effective in preventing or mitigating any attack of influenza. The producers of these vaccines know that they are worthless, but they go on selling them anyway."*

The Bottom Line: Modern Medicine vs. Natural Healing
The bottom line is that I don't advocate flu shots and never have. First, you're injecting toxic poison and animal pus into your body, and second, there is no proof at all that they're effective. And that's even from the medical authorities that are suggesting them, whether it's the FDA or the CDC.

In this new era of medicine, of Natural Medicine and Herbal Medicine, instead of using poisonous toxic chemicals with their many dangerous side effects, we need to start helping and supporting our body's own natural defense mechanisms, by boosting up our immune system, which will effectively kill off any cold or influenza.

My Personal History with Influenza
The 1957 Asian Flu Epidemic
Viruses Are KILLERS! Never underestimate their LETHAL potential…

When I was only 5 years old in 1957, I almost died from the Asian Influenza pandemic. It was a bad one and killed over 70,000 Americans, over DOUBLE the deaths than the usual seasonal influenza. It hit my area worse than the Polio epidemic.

Many kids and older folk in my little rural town didn't make it through that winter alive. I had very high fevers and the influenza eventually turned into bronchial pneumonia. I remember being delirious for days. I have only a few memories from that very early period of my life, but in my mind I can still to this day remember opening up my eyes, being very ill, and seeing a very worried look on my father's eyes. And, he NEVER looked worried. A few years later, he told me that I almost died that winter. Later on in life, it was discovered that these high fevers and the numerous drugs and vaccines I received to try and control the fevers is what partially contributed to the scarring of my already deformed heart valves.

The Spanish Influenza

I gained even more respect for viruses from my Uncle Bill. He was one of my favorite uncles and he was actually old enough to be my grandfather. See, my mother was the youngest of 16 children, so she had brothers and sisters more than 30 years older than her. Some were born before the turn of the century and her brother Bill was the oldest.

My Uncle Bill fought in both the Spanish American War with Teddy Roosevelt and also in the trenches of World War I. He was a very tough old guy, a horse soldier and definitely politically incorrect even for the 1950s. I remember I used to sit on his lap where he would roll a cigarette and light it with one hand, hold me with the other, and tell me endless hours of war stories, like the time his ship sank, flooding fast, and he had to escape from seven decks below sea level. He also had numerous other stories like the horrors of the gas attacks and brutal hand-to-hand trench fighting he saw in France.

He was the coolest guy to a little boy. He had been shell-shocked so many times that his hair was white. He had little hearing left and had numerous battle scars that he used to show me. I once asked him what was the scariest of all of his experiences? I was very surprised at his answer.

He told me that the German infantry often piled up dead American soldiers as a blockade to the advancing American soldiers. He said that it was a very gruesome sight and horrible having to climb over your friends' dead bodies, blood and guts to reach the enemy. But, he said that when he returned from war the dead bodies were piled up even higher on the docks in New York City and in the streets of America from the influenza deaths. He told me that was the scariest for a tough soldier like him—the invisible enemy.

My Uncle Bill was the last of a dying breed of horse soldiers, and he wasn't scared of anyone. He had been shot and hit with shrapnel so many times it didn't even slow him down, but the enemy he couldn't see and didn't know how to fight was the scariest one of all. I could tell by the look on his face that what he saw upon his return from war in the streets of America, the hundreds of bodies piled high and thousands dying in the street, without a shot being fired, was the scariest killer he ever saw.

Spanish Influenza Facts:

▶ The pandemic lasted two years.

▶ 100 MILLION died—over 5% of the entire world's population (more than the "Black Death Plague").

▶ 500 MILLION (one-third of the world's population) got sick.

▸ It killed mostly healthy young adults, in their 20s and 30s.

▸ It killed 1 MILLION people per week for the first 25 weeks, then it got worse…

▸ The second "wave" was much worse, also killing children and the elderly.

▸ It killed entire populations of villages. From extremely remote Arctic Villages and South Pacific Islands, entire populations of villages were discovered dead.

▸ It was one of the deadliest natural disasters in human history

Influenza Pandemics:

Spanish Influenza	1918 to 1920
Asian Influenza	1957
Hong Kong Influenza	1968

Up until now, the biggest time gap between Influenza Pandemics has been 37 years. It has been 42 years since the last Influenza Pandemic, and most scientists say we are overdue for the "big one".

Cold, Flu and Immune Glossary:

Adenoids

Also called the pharyngeal tonsils, they are a collection of lymphatic tissue on the wall of the recess of the part of the pharynx (the nasopharynx) situated above the soft palate of the mouth.

Antigen

A protein or oligosaccharide marker on the surface of cells that identifies the cell as self or non-self. This marker also identifies the type of cell, such as a heart cell or a brain cell. An antigen stimulates B-lymphocytes to produce antibodies to neutralize or destroy the cell if necessary. It also stimulates cytotoxic responses (kills cells) by granulocytes, monocytes and lymphocytes.

Antibody

Any of the complex glycoproteins produced by B-lymphocytes in response to the presence of an antigen designed to destroy or kill the antigen, providing protection against most common infections.

Appendix

The hollow, worm-shaped organ attached to the cecum (the first part of the large intestine). It has well-formed lymphoid follicles. It, as well as that of the tonsils and the Peyer's Patches in the small intestine make up a separate interconnected secretory immune system in which cells circulate which produce the protective antibodies IgA and IgE. These antibodies protect a wide area of the bowel from antigens.

This system is called MALT (short for mucosal-associated lymphoid tissue).

B-cell

A lymphoid stem cell produced in the bone marrow, but it is unknown where it is "educated". It is named after the "educator" organ in birds, (the Bursa of Fabriscus). When a B-cell comes in contact with an antigen, it turns into a plasma cell or memory cell, which produces antibodies using its surface immunoglobulin, which attach to and destroy the antigen.

Basophil

A white blood cell whose large basophilic granules contain heparin and vasoactive amines, which are important in the inflammatory response.

Bone marrow

A soft organic material that fills the interior cavities of the bone, especially the large bones such as the femur and the vertebrae. It is the site where all the types of blood cells are made.

Carcinogen

A substance that is known to cause cancer.

Carcinogenic

Causes cancer.

Chicken Pox

A highly contagious illness caused by a virus that develops into an itchy rash and red spots/blisters all over their body Common in children, most people will get it at some point in their life.

CSF

Colony stimulating factor(s); substances produced by various kinds of cells, required for the development of in vitro clones. There are also inhibitory factors, possibly including interferon.

Dysplasia

Abnormal development of tissue. Abnormal changes in the tissue as a protection mechanism against a long-term source of chronic irritation.

Epidemic

A widespread outbreak of an infectious disease (like influenza) where many people are infected at the same time.

Eosinophil

A white blood cell with large refractile eosinophilic granules, phagocytic and perhaps cytotoxic for some larger parasites, such as worms. It may also regulate the inflammatory response.

Erythroid stem cell

Cell destined to differentiate into erythrocytes (red blood cells).

Erythropoietin

A glycoprotein hormone formed in the kidney in response to hypoxia (lack of oxygen), which speeds up the differentiation of erythrocyte precursors, and thus adjusts the production of red blood cells to the demand for their oxygen-carrying capacity.

Fever

A rise in temperature in the body that indicates you are fighting an infection.

German Measles

(See Rubella.)

Granulocyte stem cell

A cell that produces granulocytes that are capable of differentiation into either neutrophils or basophils.

Hematopoietic stem cell   The precursor of all red blood cells, blood platelets, monocytes and macrophages, and all granulocyte white blood cells.

Immunoglobulin   There are five types known, referred to as IgA, IgD, IgE, IgG and IgM. They are a family of closely related proteins capable of acting as antibodies. All antibodies are immunoglobulins, however, it is not known whether all immunoglobulins act as antibodies.

Lymph nodes   Collection of lymph tissue found at intervals along the course of the lymph vessels throughout the body. The white blood cells contained in the node begin the process of inflammation and the immune attack against foreign substances.

Lymphatic system   The system that includes all the lymph vessels that collect tissue fluid and return it to the blood through the lymph capillaries, lacteals, larger vessels, the thoracic duct and the right lymphatic duct. It also includes the organs made up of lymphatic tissue (lymph nodes and nodules, the spleen, appendix, tonsils and the thymus) that produce lymphocytes and monocytes, which defend against pathogens and provide immunity.

Lymphocyte   A type of white blood cell. Subtypes: T-cells (helper, suppressor, killer, etc.) and B-cells.

Lymphoma

Cancer of the lymph nodes.

Macrophage

The main resident phagocytic white blood cell located in the tissues of the body and serous cavities such as the pleura (lining of the lungs) and peritoneum (lining of the abdominal wall) that attack and digest foreign material by phagocytosis.

Mast cell

A large tissue cell similar in appearance and function to the basophil, but thought not to originate from the bone marrow. Mast cells are easily triggered by tissue damage to begin the inflammatory response.

Measles

A highly contagious infection that causes a rash all over the body. Other symptoms include high fever, sore throat and cough.

Megakaryocyte

The parent cell of the blood platelets.

Meningitis

A contagious infection of coverings around the brain and spinal cord, and which is common in children, teens and young adults. Symptoms can include stiff/painful neck, fever, headache, vomiting, trouble staying awake and seizures.

Metastasis

Movement of cancer cells from one part of the body to another. The malignant cells may spread through the lymphatic circulation, the bloodstream, other ways such as through the cerebrospinal fluid.

Monocyte

The largest nucleated cell of the blood, developing into a macrophage when it migrates into the tissues.

Mumps

A contagious infection in the salivary glands located in the side of the face or below the ears. You might have flu-like symptoms, abdominal pain or swollen cheeks.

Myeloid stem cell

The precursor of monocyte and macrophage white blood cells.

Neutrophils

The most common type of white blood cell also called a polymorph. It is a short-lived phagocytic cell whose granules contain numerous substances, which kill bacteria.

Pandemic

A widespread outbreak of an infectious disease where people in a region, continent or throughout the world are infected at the same time.

Pathogen

A micro-organism or substance capable of producing a disease, a germ that can be virus, bacteria, fungus, etc.

Peyer's patches

A part of your immune system, a collection of lymph nodules found mainly in mucous membrane lining the ileum of the small intestine near where it joins with the large intestine. They are circular or oval, about half an inch wide and an inch in length.

Phagocyte | A cell that ingests and digests virus, bacteria and pathogens through the process of phagocytosis.

Plasma cell | A B-cell in its high-rate antibody secreting state. Despite their name, plasma cells are seldom seen in the blood, but are found in the spleen, lymph nodes, etc. Basically, wherever antibodies are being made.

Pneumonia | A virus that causes one or both lungs get inflamed. People with pneumonia can have difficulty breathing, a cough or fever.

Red blood cells | The cells in the blood that give it its characteristic red color. Red blood cells contain hemoglobin (an iron-rich substance), which carry oxygen.

Rubella | Caused by the Rubella virus, which is mild and not long-term. It is more dangerous to pregnant women, who can transfer this virus to their unborn child, causing possible birth defects.

Sinus | Your sinuses are in your skull and they drain into your nose. Their job is to clear your head.

Sinus Infection | Also known as Sinusitis, it is a swelling of the tissue around the sinuses. Instead of air circulating through them, sinuses are blocked with fluid and germs, which can cause an infection.

Stem cell

The original cell made in the Bone Marrow that transforms into all the types of red and white blood cells.

Strep Throat

An illness caused by a bacterial infection in your throat and tonsils. Throat gets highly irritated, causing extreme soreness, fever and white spots at the back of a very red throat.

T-cell

A lymphoid cell that travels to the thymus gland where it develops into a mature lymphocyte that circulates between the blood and the lymph. T-cells fight mainly against viruses, fungi and cancer cells. T-cells are covered by surface protein markers (called CD proteins), which identify the cell. Subtypes of T-cells include "helper", "suppressor" and "killer" T-cells.

Thrombopoietin

Hormone that regulates the production of platelets.

Thymus

Lymphoid organ located just above and in front of the heart. The thymus is essential to the maturation of the thymic lymphoid cells, called T-cells. Removal of the thymus during early childhood has been associated with an increased susceptibility to acute infectious diseases later on in life.

Tonsils

Usually refers to the palatine tonsils—a collection of lymphatic tissue located at the back of the throat on either side in depressions of the mucous membrane.

The tonsil produces lymphocytes and monocytes and contains macrophages that engulf and destroy pathogens that get through the epithelium. There are also the lingual tonsils, which lie at the back of the tongue, and the pharyngeal tonsils (adenoids).

Tonsillitis

An inflammation of the tonsils that is typically caused by an infection. Symptoms can include sore throat, trouble swallowing and fever.

Uvula

A piece of tissue found in the back of the throat, which can be seen when you open the mouth wide. Its purpose is to keep food from going down your breathing passage when swallowing.

White blood cells

Cells in the blood that make up the immune system.